MODERN FIDELITY CLAIM DESKBOOK

Understanding the Impact of Technology

SARAH R. CLARK, THERESA A. GOOLEY,
AND TONI SCOTT REED, EDITORS

ABA
AMERICAN BAR ASSOCIATION
Tort Trial and Insurance
Practice Section

Printed in the United States of America.

29 28 27 26 25 5 4 3 2 1

ISBN: 978-1-63905-710-8

ISSN: 1543-9305-711-5

Table of Contents

Preface

This all-new Modern Fidelity Claim Deskbook was inspired by technology and the criminals that perpetually look for ways to cause loss to businesses with increased speed, volume, and anonymity. Technology changes our lives and businesses every day. So too does it change fidelity and crime claims, requiring insurance companies and insureds to adapt, understand current risks, and prepare for high-tech losses.

Case law has been quickly developing and changing in the context of claims involving technology-based losses. Professionals must, therefore, have command of not only the law but also the developing crime and cyber insurance products on the market and the technical vocabulary necessary to understand modern claims and claim facts.

The Deskbook was born out of the need for a practical guide to handling computer-related claims. Because technology has driven the types of coverage offered in modern fidelity bonds and crime policies, we thought that a hands-on guide addressing both coverage issues and real-world business technology under one cover could be a critical resource. These materials take a slightly different approach—compared to earlier scholarly works—by providing a framework of practical information to apply in the technology context.

THE MODERN FIDELITY CLAIM DESKBOOK: UNDERSTANDING THE IMPACT OF TECHNOLOGY can be a starting point to understand and analyze complex issues and underlying technology. We hope that it becomes a trusted companion for professionals involved in fidelity and crime claims.

It has been a privilege to design and implement the concept for an entirely new Fidelity & Surety Law Committee book. We thank Bruce L. Corriveau, the 2025-26 Chair of the FSLC, for embracing this book and featuring it as the subject matter for the FSLC Fall Fidelity Conference held in Chicago, Illinois, from October 9-10, 2025.

SARAH R. CLARK
THERESA A. GOOLEY
TONI SCOTT REED
Book Developers
September 2025

Introduction

Crime in the business context is old, recurring, and (it seems) impossible to completely eliminate. Fidelity bonds and crime policies exist in that reality. The Financial Institution Bond, Standard Form No. 24, had its genesis in 1916, when various types of coverages for financial institutions were combined into a single policy. The various types of commercial crime policies available for commercial businesses are also many decades-old. The original iteration of these products occupied a time of paper-based transactions and face-to-face relationships.

Today's business environment relies upon technology to do things faster, more efficiently, and more profitably. With the addition of technology has come the addition of technology-driven criminal activity. As fidelity bonds and crime policies have adapted with the times, so too must fidelity claims handers, underwriters, consultants, experts, and outside counsel. That development depends on both an in-depth understanding of the nature and extent of fidelity bond and crime policy coverages and keen insight into how technologically-based systems function; their functions, benefits, and risks; and how they might be used in ways that implicate—or fail to trigger—coverage under fidelity bonds and crime policies.

While staying abreast of the pace of technological advancements may seem daunting, the chapters featured in this Deskbook endeavor to provide a resource for the broad base of knowledge required to capably evaluate coverage for technology-based schemes for all practitioners—whether just beginning a career in fidelity or developing expertise built over decades. The topics range from advising on of-the-moment legal decisions applying insuring agreements to technology-driven crimes to explaining how computer systems and related components operate, from outlining current technology-based crimes to breaking down how they are perpetrated.

Some chapters of the Deskbook focus on specific coverage available in fidelity bonds and crime policies, others focus on computer systems and security, and still others are a combination of both subject matters. The Table of Contents is designed to assist the reader in locating details in each chapter that may be of interest in a particular inquiry.

Finally, this Deskbook is also designed to function as a practical companion to THE FINANCIAL INSTITUTION BOND AND COMMERCIAL CRIME POLICY: PRINCIPLES AND ANNOTATIONS, published by the Fidelity & Surety Law Committee in 2023. That encyclopedic resource provides a comprehensive discussion of the case law and secondary sources relevant to all aspects of fidelity bonds and crime policies, while the Deskbook provides a technology-specific set of materials focusing on the ways computers and technology are influencing coverage provided by fidelity bonds and crime policies.

On behalf of the Fidelity & Surety Law Committee, we want to thank each of the authors for their significant contributions to this important project. It has been a real privilege to combine the ideas and the talents of legal experts, accounting and forensic experts, and technology experts to produce the content of the Deskbook. The authors' depth of knowledge and expertise, their generosity of spirit, and their interest in promoting the cause of the Fidelity & Surety Law Committee, are evident in their work.

Additionally, we extend a special thank you to Debbie Avery, in Clark Hill's word processing department, for her hours of work to prepare, revise, format, and triple check the camera-ready art used for publication of this book. We are grateful to you, Debbie, and we are likewise grateful for the opportunity to work together on this project.

SARAH R. CLARK
THERESA A. GOOLEY
TONI SCOTT REED
Editors
September 2025

Contributors

EDITORS

SARAH R. CLARK • Vice President of Fidelity Claims, Financial Lines Claims with American International Group (AIG). Ms. Clark is a graduate of the University of Illinois (B.A. 2010) and Wake Forest University School of Law (J.D. 2013).

THERESA A. GOOLEY • Managing Director & Counsel, Bond & Specialty Insurance, with Travelers. Ms. Gooley is a graduate of the University of Minnesota (B.S. 1990) and Drake University Law School (J.D. 1994).

TONI SCOTT REED • Member in Clark Hill PLC. Ms. Reed is a graduate of Southern Methodist University (B.B.A. and B.A. *summa cum laude* 1990, and the Southern Methodist University Dedman School of Law (J.D. *cum laude* 1993). She is a Past Chair of the Fidelity & Surety Law Committee of the American Bar Association, Tort Trial and Insurance Practice Section. She is Co-Chair of the Book Publishing Board and Vice Chair of the Cybersecurity & Data Privacy Committee of the American Bar Association, Tort Trial and Insurance Practice Section.

AUTHORS

CHRISTOPER BALLOD • Partner in Mullen Coughlin. Mr. Ballod is a graduate of Pennsylvania State University (B.A) and Widener University Delaware Law School (J.D.).

CHRISTIE M. BIRD • Partner in Frenkel Lambert Weisman & Gordon, LLP. Ms. Bird is a graduate of Gonzaga University (B.A. 1997) and Temple University Beasley School of Law (J.D. 2000). She is a member of the Book Publishing Board of the American Bar Association, Tort Trial and Insurance Practice Section.

JENNIFER BOLLINGER • Vice-President—Commercial Crime Product Specialist at Old Republic Professional. Ms. Bollinger is a graduate of the University of Illinois Urbana-Champaign (B.A. 2003).

CARLETON R. BURCH • Partner in Anderson, McPharlin & Conners, LLP. Mr. Burch is a graduate of Colorado College (B.A. *cum laude*, 1984) and the University of California Law School—San Francisco (J.D. 1987).

ANDY J. CHAMBERS • Partner in Jennings Haug Keleher McLeod Waterfall LLP. Mr. Chambers is a graduate of the University of California (B.A. 1999) and American University Washington College of Law (J.D. *cum laude, with honors* 2004).

J. CARALISA CONNELL • Partner in The Dry Law Firm. Ms. Connell is a graduate of the University of Louisville (B.S. 2014) and Belmont University College of Law (J.D. *magna cum laude* 2017). She is a Vice Chair of the Fidelity & Surety Law Committee of the American Bar Association, Tort Trial & Insurance Practice Section, as well as Co-Chair of its Technology Subcommittee and Co-Chair of its Young Professionals Subcommittee.

ADAM P. FRIEDMAN • Member in Chiesa Shahinian & Giantomasi PC. Mr. Friedman is a graduate of Cornell University (B.S. 1988) and Yeshiva University Benjamin N. Cardozo School of Law (J.D. 1991). He is a past chair of the Fidelity & Surety Law Committee of the American Bar Association, Tort Trial and Insurance Practice Section.

C. CLARK HODGSON III • Partner in Jennings Haug Keleher McLeod Waterfall LLP. Mr. Hodgson is a graduate of the University of Scranton (B.S. 2010) and Rutgers School of Law-Camden (J.D. 2013). Mr. Hodgson is a member of the 2025-26 Emerging Leaders Class of the Fidelity & Surety Law Committee of the American Bar Association, Tort Trial and Insurance Practice Section.

MARK KRONE • Director, Senior Claim Counsel, Bond & Specialty with Travelers. Mr. Lippe is a graduate of the University of Colorado (B.S. 1989) and Fordham University School of Law (J.D. 1995).

JOHN W. LIPPE • Director, Cyber Claim Forensics, Bond & Specialty with Travelers. Mr. Lippe is a graduate of Porter and Chester Technical Institute (A.S. 1986).

JUAN B. MARTINEZ • Vice President at LFI FALS, LLC. Mr. Martinez is a graduate of Hunter College (B.S. 2005).

KATHERINE MUSBACH • Partner in Gordon Rees Scully Mansukhani, LLP. Ms. Musbach is a graduate of the University of Michigan (B.A. *with distinction and highest honors* 2008) and Duke University (J.D. *cum laude* 2013).

TONI SCOTT REED • Member in Clark Hill PLC. Ms. Reed is a graduate of Southern Methodist University (B.B.A. and B.A. *summa cum laude* 1990, and the Dedman School of Law of Southern Methodist University (J.D. *cum laude* 1993). She is a Past Chair of the Fidelity & Surety Law Committee of the American Bar Association, Tort Trial and Insurance Practice Section. She is Co-Chair of the Book Publishing Board and Vice Chair of the Cybersecurity & Data Privacy Committee of the American Bar Association, Tort Trial and Insurance Practice Section.

JONATHAN RAJEWSKI • Vice President Forensic Services Practice--Charles River Associates. Mr. Rajewski is a graduate of Hilbert College (B.S. 2004) and Champlain College (M.S. 2009).

BRIAN RICE • Chief Executive Officer at RiskScape Strategies, LLC. Mr. Rice is a graduate of the University of Texas at Austin (B.S. 2022). He is a Co-Chair of the Technology Subcommittee of the Fidelity & Surety Law Committee of the American Bar Association, Tort Trial & Insurance Practice Section.

CAROL Z. SMITH • Shareholder/Director in Dysart Taylor Cotter McMonigle & Brummitt, P.C. Ms. Smith is a graduate of the University of Kansas (B.A. 1984) and the University of Kansas School of Law (J.D. 1987). She is a Past Chair of the Fidelity & Surety Law Committee of the American Bar Association, Tort Trial and Insurance Practice Section.

IGA TODD • Partner in Gordon Rees Scully Mansukhani, LLP. Ms. Todd is a graduate of the University of Illinois (B.S. 2012) and the University of Wisconsin (J.D. 2015).

JESSE YANCO • Associate in Anderson, McPharlin & Conners, LLP. Mr. Yanco is a graduate of California State University, Chico (B.A. 2010) and Gonzaga University School of Law (J.D. *cum laude* 2014).

CHAPTER 1

THEFT AND TECHNOLOGY'S ROLE IN MODERN CRIME LOSSES AND CLAIM INVESTIGATIONS

Christie M. Bird
Juan B. Martinez

I. Introduction

The use of technology in the commission of theft in the workplace and other commercial settings is nothing new. For as long as companies have been using computers and electronic communication systems to conduct business, opportunities for committing theft against those companies with the aid of technology abound. However, fidelity and other crime claims demonstrate that the use of technology to commit theft has become increasingly more sophisticated and organized, and is making theft easier to commit and scale. This chapter addresses the ways in which technology is being used by insiders and outsiders in modern crime claims and how professionals involved in investigating and evaluating these claims can use some basic technologies to make the performance of their own work in the claims investigation process more efficient.

II. Tech-Enabled Theft and Fraud in Crime Claim Losses

Traditional fidelity claims readily trigger visions of an employee stealing inventory, committing check fraud, submitting inflated expense reports, or engaging in vendor invoice kickback schemes. These classic theft schemes still occur in a largely non-digital manner—e.g., stealing product from a warehouse, altering or forging paper checks, or simply approving payment of fraudulently-inflated invoices. The modern crime claims that we review, however, often involve some kind of fraudulent computer-based activity, whether by insiders or outsiders, or both. These include claims resulting from sending fraudulent communications by email, to exploiting the newest technologies that automate the fraud, and which or may not be directly responsible for the losses experienced by the insured.

A. Manipulation of Financial and Inventory Systems

The digital nature of modern business operations combined with poor or non-existent internal controls provides bad actor employees with easier ways to commit and conceal their fraud against their employers. The fraudulent use of an insured's electronic payroll systems is just one example. This claim scenario may involve an employee with authority to access the insured's payroll system, increasing his or her own salary or wages or paying unauthorized bonuses. It may also involve an authorized employee failing to remove departing employees from the payroll system, updating the departing employee's W-4 forms to include the bad actor employee's address, routing and checking account number, or adding "ghost" or fictitious employees to the insured's payroll system, resulting in a loss to the insured of not only the wages paid to the non-existent employees, but also other costs associated with the employment relationship.

Unauthorized use of insureds' other financial systems and inventory systems also occurs. A typical claim scenario may involve an employee using his or her access to the insured's system to conceal the theft committed. They may do this by shifting the cost of the stolen inventory from the actual project or profit center, to an unrelated, more profitable project or profit center, or removing or writing off the stolen inventory from the system all together. Or, an employee may fraudulently alter financial data, not to commit or conceal theft, but to mask poor performance in some part of the insured's business, resulting in payment by the insured of performance-based bonuses and other remuneration not *actually* earned, whether or not such payments were intended by the dishonest employee, and which the insured may contend is a covered employee theft loss. With these types of claims, the use of the insured's systems and manipulation of data does not cause the loss, or directly cause the loss, but is a means used to facilitate the employee's conduct.

B. ACH Fraud

While check fraud is still a regular occurrence in crime claims, claims for ACH fraud have been increasing. Broadly, ACH fraud is any fraudulent transfer of funds between bank accounts over the Automated Clearing House network. The ACH network has been in existence since the early 1970s and was created with the intention of replacing the use of paper checks.[1] By 2008, the commercial ACH volume processed by the Federal Reserve (10 billion transactions annually) overtook check volumes for the first time.[2] The entire ACH process, from the initiation of the payment to processing and full settlement of the transactions, evolved such that it now occurs in a completely automated fashion.

Claims for fraudulent ACH debit transactions by unknown bad actors appear to be increasing with their potential for massive losses with little effort. "Pull fraud" in the context of ACH refers to a type of unauthorized or fraudulent ACH debit where a bad actor "pulls" money from a victim's bank account without permission. Some insureds are claiming that bad actors merely need access to the insured's bank account number and routing number to enable them to debit money out of the insured's account. This is especially concerning given the relative availability of such banking information to insiders and outsiders, including anyone who has ever had access to a check drawn on the insured's account or who is employed by organizations that have ever made an ACH payment to the insured. It takes just one bad actor to obtain an insured's banking information and publish it on the internet for widespread disclosure and fraud.

Another area of ACH fraud appearing in crime claims is ACH kiting, the modern equivalent of check kiting. Like check kiting, ACH kiting generally involves a bad actor fraudulently initiating an electronic transfer from an insufficiently funded account at one bank to an account at a different bank, and then withdrawing the funds while the ACH is being processed and before the funds have fully settled in the recipient account. This lag time is typically 1-3 business days in a standard ACH transaction, during which the recipient account reflects a temporary inflated balance that includes the pending funds that have not yet actually been received, and thereby permitting the bad actor to withdraw funds that do not actually

---

1. *See* NACHA.org homepage.
2. *See* www.federalreservehistory.org homepage.

exist. As with check kiting, the bad actor may repeat the cycle with back-and-forth movements of funds between the ACH accounts.

Although ACH kiting and check kiting are similar, ACH kiting arguably may pose the greater threat. A check's lag time (or "float") normally takes longer than ACH lag time, especially for traditional paper checks which require being physically handled and possibly mailed. Check kiting requires the creation of a fraudulent check whereas ACH is automated. Thus, the faster speed and automation of ACH transactions could be more appealing to bad actors who want to quickly repeat the cycle of fraudulent transfers back and forth between accounts. In addition, banks' use of check "holds," a loss/fraud mitigation tool, may also push bad actors toward ACH over checks because it adds a delay before any funds are made available for withdrawal to provide time for the bank to ensure that the check is valid and that the payor's account has sufficient funds.

C. Business Email Compromise

Social engineering is an umbrella term for a variety of cyberfraud that manipulates people into disclosing confidential information and login credentials or taking action, like transferring money. Social engineering occurs in a host of variations, but the dominant social engineering tactic appearing in crime claims remains business email compromise ("BEC"). In BECs, a bad actor sends an email to an employee of an insured while pretending to be a trusted person, such as an executive of the organization or a vendor or a client the insured has an established relationship with, and instructs the employee to change the bank account information on file for the impersonated individual or organization, or requests payment from the insured. This generally occurs in one of two ways. The first is where the bad actor gains unauthorized access to the email account of the individual they are impersonating and sends the fraudulent email from that person's account. In the other, the bad actor sends the fraudulent email from a "spoofed" email account, which has an email address that differs from the real email address of the impersonated individual but is similar enough to go unnoticed. In both scenarios, the target employees within the organization ultimately follow the bad actor's request and voluntarily initiate payment of the insured's funds to the bad actor's account.

Social engineering occurred in the pre-digital era, but impersonations happened over the phone, by correspondence sent through the mail, or in person. Modern social engineering fraud allows bad actors to conceal themselves behind electronic communications and exploits all the bad habits we have developed in communicating electronically. Critically, the social engineering scams of today rely on our tendency not to pay close attention to the digital clues that give the scam away, such as the sender's email address or web page URLs. Today's social engineering scams count on our tendency to mindlessly and automatically click weblinks and open attachments presented to us.

These scams are well-known to the general public, yet they are still effective. According to the FBI, in 2024 alone, BEC scams accounted for more than 21,400 complaints received and more than $2.7 billion in transfers.[3] From 2022 to 2024, BECs accounted for more than 64,700 complaints received and nearly $8.5 billion in transfers.[4] Unsurprisingly, social engineering claims have become one of, if not the, most common type of claims in carriers' crime book.

D. Deepfakes

Crime claims allegedly involving the fraudulent use of real time "deepfake" videoconferences and phone calls have arisen in the past few years. Deepfakes are synthetic media, typically videos or audio, created using artificial intelligence (AI) techniques, particularly deep learning, to manipulate or generate realistic-looking content that appears authentic but is fabricated or altered. More broadly, videos and audio that are "deepfake" swap an image of a person with someone else's image and the voice of a person with someone else's voice. Trained on legitimate images, video footage, and audio of the real person, the AI learns the person's physical features, voice, and mannerisms and that learning can be used to generate videos and audio of individuals doing and saying things they did not actually do or say, like instructing their target to make a payment to a new account.

To the extent "deepfake" videoconferences and audio are used to deceive an insured into transferring money or property to a bad actor, they boil down to social engineering fraud that is no different than, for instance, a BEC. But in our view, "deepfake" technology merits special attention because of its ability to generate such high-quality impersonations in recordings and videoconferences and calls and to mislead diligent insureds

3. Federal Bureau of Investigation 2024 IC3 Annual Report, at 9-10, 18-19.
4. *Id.*

into believing a transaction is properly authenticated through a call-back or similar verification method which, when used correctly, would often prevent a BEC loss from occurring in the first instance. Unlike BECs, deepfakes may leave no obvious digital clues that the communication is a fraud to a layperson. And as companies have become more accustomed to conducting business and meetings remotely by videoconferencing since the COVID-19 pandemic, the opportunities for deepfakes to deceive organizations into causing their own financial loss are greater than ever. In short, we anticipate that deepfake technology may increase the efficacy of BEC tactics, as unwitting recipients may identify no red flags and see no reason to question the authenticity of a conversation they have just had, face-to-face or voice-to-voice, with someone they recognize.

E. Computer Hacking

Claims for losses caused by breaches of an insured's computer system still occur, but they tend to appear more often in combination with social engineering fraud. In these scenarios, the targeted employee unwittingly opens the door for the bad actor to infiltrate systems used by the insured to steal. For example, a bad actor may send an email to an employee of an insured that contains a malicious attachment (e.g., PDF, Word document) disguised as an invoice or résumé, for instance, while purporting to be a known entity or person. This can be particularly harmful because attachments can contain malware that is installed on the insured's system when opened. Malware is malicious software or code that can be designed to cause a wide variety of harms, just one of which is giving the bad actor remote access to the target's computer system to steal information or manipulate data. Alternatively, the bad actor may send an email that contains a malicious, embedded link. When the target employee clicks the link, they can be directed to a fake website that looks legitimate enough for the employee to voluntarily disclose confidential information. Or, the employee can be directed to a cloned login page that looks identical to a login page the insured normally uses albeit with a different URL. Because a cloned page interacts with the real page, when the employee logs in with their username and password, they give the bad actor access to the real page. The bad actors are not only imposters, they deceive their targets into giving them the information and access that allows them to steal.

F. Algorithms and Bots

Crime claims are increasingly being presented under the assumption (by insureds or their forensic investigators) that bad actors used algorithms and bots to learn the private information of insureds or their customers to steal from them. Algorithms are a set of instructions used in computing which are designed to solve a problem or accomplish a task. Bots are software applications that perform tasks in an automated fashion. Because both methods essentially automate the work required of bad actors to steal valuable information and can be scaled, algorithms and bots pose a potentially significant risk for little effort. In that way, they are increasingly attractive to bad actors attempting to cast a wide net.

An example of such claims are those where bad actors obtain account numbers, payment card numbers, or merchant gift card numbers belonging to customers of the insured to make fraudulent purchases. The assumption that algorithms and bots were used to discover the account number sequences or gift card number sequences and to make purchases using those account/gift card numbers is often premised upon the high volume of impacted accounts and gift cards, the high volume of unauthorized transactions, and/or the wide geographical location of the purchases in the given loss period. In short, the scale of the fraud could only have been achieved by the automation that algorithms and bots provide.

Algorithms and bots have also been used to perpetrate brute force attacks. For example, a claim may be submitted alleging a bad actor obtained access to an administrative account through a brute force attack designed to guess different login credentials until happening upon the correct password. Once in the system with administrative access, bad actors can process transactions or uncover critical information about an insured's business and operations.

G. Weaknesses in Software

Modern crime claims also demonstrate how bad actors exploit weaknesses in insureds' own software to commit fraud without breaching any system. For example, bad actors have targeted insureds who sell products that require a digital or telephone redemption or activation prior to use, such as gift cards and pre-paid debit cards. In these schemes, bad actors identify those systems that have a gap or flaw in their design which permits multiple, simultaneous activations of the same product where only a single activation or redemption was purchased. These automated systems do not account for *simultaneous* redemptions and process the transactions without recognizing the fraud. To compound the issue, where this exploitation of the insured's software weakness is powered by algorithms and bots, the potential to quickly scale the fraudulent redemptions across a large volume of products is even more significant.

Bad actors have also exploited system weaknesses in e-lending or credit application schemes. In such schemes, a single bad actor or group of bad actors working together may submit a mass of credit card or loan applications through an online website. Where such websites rely primarily on automated review and approval processes, bad actors may exploit weaknesses in the security or risk-appetite settings to obtain approval for a large amount of fraudulent cards or loans, which are then used to make fraudulent purchases or the proceeds transferred to other accounts. Such schemes may take time for the insured to identify the suspicious accounts or identify their similarities and connection to each other. That time favors the bad actors, who may be able to accomplish a large theft in a relatively short period of time until the weakness is identified and addressed.

III.
Technology Available for the Review of Crime Claims

For professionals involved in investigating or evaluating claims, it is helpful to stay ahead of technological trends. We address some basic tools, among the vast products available in the marketplace, that claims professionals, forensic accountants/consultants, and coverage counsel are using or could employ to be more efficient in their work and, perhaps, to better understand the crime claims presented.

A. Open Source Intelligence (OSINT)

Open source intelligence is a fancy term for the process of collecting and analyzing publicly available information for investigations. This includes social media, websites, public records, news articles, government databases, and other open sources. Open source intelligence helps to corroborate or dispute statements made by insureds and their investigation findings. Examples of reliable open source intelligence that can be useful to a claims examiner, counsel, or accountant include:

- LinkedIn: A professional social networking platform utilized by many professionals for networking with colleagues, clients and potential clients, employers and business partners. When presented with a fidelity claim, it is standard to search for the subject principal on LinkedIn to see how they represent their work history, education, skills, etc., and how that information compares to the information contained in their personnel file maintained by the insured employer and statements in the insured's forensic investigation reports. When discrepancies are found, insurance professionals can discuss with the insured to gain a better understanding of whether the work history posted on LinkedIn is inaccurate. LinkedIn can also be useful for tracking the whereabouts of a former employee after their separation from the insured if recovery efforts are being contemplated.
- Government databases: Such state and business registries may allow a clams professional to confirm whether the entities involved are real or fictitious companies or to obtain the registered agent of an organization. Regulators' databases, such as FINRA BrokerCheck, provide information on brokers, and brokerage firms, including any complaints or disciplinary actions against them. The Securities and Exchange Commission maintains copies of public filings related to a large number of companies falling within its purview, including regulatory filings and disclosures reported in Form 10-Ks, 10-Qs, or 8-Ks.
- Newspaper articles: The New York Times, Wall Street Journal, and other publications report on significant news of the day like large scale data breaches, fraud disclosed by whistleblowers and insider tips, regulatory filings and disclosures, and court records and lawsuits. Local news outlets should be consulted to identify information relevant to a claim, including whether the claimed theft was publicly reported, whether arrests have been made, and the progress of civil or criminal proceedings related to same.

In addition to the above resources, there is also a benefit to simply crafting a few searches in your favorite search engine to find out more about the insured's business or relevant location, an alleged dishonest employee or third party thief, or the relationships between entities, some of which may or may not be insureds.

B. Large Language Models

Large language models (LLMs) are, for the purposes of this chapter, machine learning models that are trained on massive datasets (e.g., books, articles, websites, etc.) to generate human language. At a basic level, they can be useful tools for claim handlers, lawyers and forensic accountants to quickly obtain information about practically any topic. It can be helpful to ask the models about industries insureds operate within that they are unfamiliar with, about specific insureds, and even about the existence of pertinent legal authorities, etc. For example, the following queries could be posed to gain general background information in a claim investigation:

- Tell me about Company ABC.
- What industry is Company ABC in?
- In what state is Company ABC incorporated?
- What is ABC's parent company (or subsidiaries)?
- Tell me about Industry DEF.
- Tell me about any news articles about Company ABC relating to data breaches.
- Has Employee John Doe been prosecuted for XYZ against Company ABC?
- Tell me how fraudsters are committing gift card fraud?
- Have any courts interpreted the meaning of the term XYZ in a crime insurance policy?

The level of detail in the answers tends to be better when a question includes more detail. For example, when a user asks Grok the following query: "Please tell me about fraud," the answer is, obviously, broader then when the query is, "Please tell me about fraud as it relates to Deepfakes."

LLMs tailor responses over time to better respond to a user's specific needs, context, and preferences. They can also summarize and provide more polished answers about topics within a matter of seconds, a task that would otherwise take exponentially more time.

This is not to suggest that the responses provided by LLMs should automatically be accepted as accurate or truthful. LLMs are prone to "hallucinations," or instances in which they provide incorrect, misleading, or entirely fabricated information. We therefore view the use of LLMs as merely a starting point when seeking information but caution individuals to verify it through independent research and consulting source materials. For these and other reasons, users should take care to verify that the LLM's responses are accurate and have a good understanding of the subject matter before relying on the information, especially in professional work product. The same is true for search engine results where LLM-generated responses appear as the first responsive hit.

To verify the information in the LLM responses, multiple LLMs can be utilized and asked the same question, along with independent research, to check the responses. There are now several LLMs available in the market. Some of the more well-known models include ChatGPT, owned by Open AI, which appears to have been the first LLM in the marketplace when released in 2018; Gemini, owned by Google; Grok, owned by xAI (a company founded by Elon Musk in 2023); and DeepSeek, an open source model owned by the Chinese AI firm of the same name. Which is best remains subjective. However, the direct source of each model's information varies. ChatGPT has access to the Microsoft Bing browser and is utilized by Microsoft Copilot which is integrated with the various Microsoft office apps. Google Gemini has access to Google's ecosystem from Google Search, Workspace apps (Gmail, Docs, Sheets, Slides), YouTube, and other Google services for real-time information and enhanced productivity. Grok has access to the social media platform X (formerly Twitter) and the web.

Some, but not all, LLMs cite or link the source for their responses. ChatGPT, for instance, cites the websites or other sources used to formulate its answer on the face of a button that when clicked, will open a side panel with a summary from the website and a link that opens the relevant web page. Similarly, Google Gemini provides a "sources" button that when clicked, opens a side panel with relevant links to websites or other content that Gemini may have used to formulate its answer. If sources are not voluntarily provided with an answer, users can ask a follow-up question such as, "Can you cite your sources?"

Employers may have policies in place regarding the use of LLMs. Some prohibit their employees from utilizing LLMs out of a concern it could lead to intellectual property leaks or that it could create other risks relating to security, data privacy, and compliance with regulations, to name a few. However, many organizations have no policies in place regarding the use of LLMs, and users may appreciate the benefits of using LLMs but not necessarily the risks.

In short, LLMs are helpful resources with widespread use both in and out of the workplace, but the information should be independently verified before it is relied upon.

C. Digital Note Taking

Taking notes by pen and pads of paper will always have a place in certain situations, but digital note-taking applications can be a useful and efficient tool to create a record and timeline of meetings, decisions, and task responsibilities, among other things, and to organize and share this information among multiple users. These applications are generally designed to mimic a traditional notebook in a user-friendly digital space.

We use Microsoft's digital note-taking application, OneNote, as an example since Microsoft Office is the dominant suite of applications used in the insurance, legal, and accounting industries. While these workforces are all well-versed in its main applications, such as Outlook Word, Excel, and PowerPoint, they may be less familiar with OneNote and how to use it. For note-taking meetings, it is as simple as going into the Outlook calendar, clicking on the scheduled meeting, and then clicking on "Send to OneNote," which generates a summary of the scheduled meeting, including the subject header, meeting date and time, participants, a note section to add the agenda and to take notes during and after the meeting, and can include relevant attached documents for discussion. All of the information is organized and stored in one place and can be shared, reviewed and edited in real-time by multiple users who can all see the others' changes being made in real time.

In other contexts, physical devices with styluses are used in place of traditional paper notepads and pens. Depending on the particular device, such products may enable the user to convert handwritten notes to text or allow the user to add handwritten notations on uploaded pdf documents, all of which are stored in cloud-based systems. Where teams are working with each other remotely now more than ever, digital note-taking applications can be especially helpful.

D. AI Assistants

AI assistants are software applications that use artificial intelligence to understand natural language voice commands (e.g., Apple's Siri and Amazon's Alexa) or text commands (e.g., Microsoft CoPilot). They can help summarize calls, meetings, and other content. For example, Microsoft CoPilot integrates with Microsoft 365 applications. When combined with OneNote, CoPilot can summarize notes, organize text into bullet points or to do-lists, generate ideas or rewrite content more clearly. When combined with Microsoft Teams, CoPilot can transcribe calls, identify key discussion points, and sync with OneNote.

E. Videoconferencing

Prior to the COVID-19 pandemic, many professionals involved with crime insurance claims had never heard of Zoom nor used videoconferencing to any significant degree, if at all, in their jobs. Conference calls and meetings held in person were the norm. The pandemic forced a steep learning curve, resulting in what is now routine: using videoconferencing to hold meetings, conduct or appear for examination under oath's (EUO's) and depositions, attend hearings in court, and participate in mediations and arbitrations. Videoconferencing has now become so embedded in our work routines it is hard to imagine a time when we did not use it. And, if anything, videoconferencing has shown how quickly we can adapt to new technology.

During the claim investigation, videoconferencing can also assist in information sharing. The ability to share documents and discuss comments and questions in a single forum (as if in-person at a conference table) can help ensure claims handlers have the same understanding of the facts and information presented as the insured. The forum can also bring together professionals from a wide geographic area, including insured/insurer representatives, retained experts/consultants, and retained counsel, at significant cost, time, and expense savings.

IV.
Conclusion

As crime claims demonstrate, technology has given bad actors simple and sophisticated means to perpetrate theft, avenues to exploit vulnerabilities in people and systems, and the ability to carry out their fraud with anonymity, speed, and at scale. As a result, it makes sense for claims, legal, and accounting professionals to understand, and to take advantage, of the technologies that are readily available to improve efficiencies in their own work and the claims investigation process overall.

CHAPTER 2

INSURING AGREEMENTS (D) AND (E)—WHAT CONSTITUTES AN "ORIGINAL" AND RELIANCE IN THE ELECTRONIC WORLD

Iga Todd

I.
Introduction

Society's continued adoption of electronic transactions is transforming the lending industry. Electronic communications are replacing in-person meetings. Gone are the days when banking customers had to travel to a brick-and-mortar branch with physical copies of their financial documents, meet with a representative, wait weeks for a credit decision, and travel back to the branch to receive their funds.[1] Traditionally, lenders met personally with consumers to close a loan, conducting in-person closings where the borrower executed the critical loan documents before bank personnel and a notary public. Such closings provided the bank visual assurance that the borrowers had the opportunity to review the transactional documents and that the principals properly executed the loan documents. Modern-day consumers expect lenders to offer the convenience and speed afforded by digital technology—enabling them to apply for loans on their mobile devices and execute loan documents from the convenience of their home without the burden of attending an in-person closing. The convenience afforded by digital

---

1. Saurabh Singh, *Digital Transformation in Banking: What It Means for Businesses*, APPINVENTIV (Dec. 19, 2022), https://appinventiv.com/blog/digital-transformation-in-banking.

lending creates a degree of separation and anonymity increasing the risk of fraud.

Traditional lending relied on human interaction and financial underwriting to mitigate the risk of loan fraud and borrower impersonation. The lack of in-person meetings to ensure identities of signors and the proper execution of the loan documents provides fraudsters an opportunity to take advantage of digital lending and induce lenders to extend credit by impersonating borrowers and misrepresenting authority to execute loan documents. As electronic exchanges increasingly become more prevalent, financial institutions can readily fall prey to fraud and mistakenly assume the proper approval of loans and execution of loan documents.

The Financial Institution Bond covers transactions involving specifically enumerated documents bearing a qualifying impairment, but only if the insured applies traditional banking practices and obtains the original loan documents before extending credit. To that end, the Financial Institution Bond requires the insured to obtain the "original" documents and requires actual physical possession of those documents. The rationale for requiring original loan documents is to allow the insured financial institution the opportunity to inspect the documents for potential forgeries or alterations. Because electronic documents are vulnerable to manipulation (e.g., an electronic signature could be copied and pasted), the original requirement is vital to protect financial institutions from the risk of fraud. When evaluating whether the loss involved an original covered document, the claims professional must ask questions to determine the timing of the insured's receipt of the document.

II.
Coverage Under Insuring Agreements (D) and (E) of A Standard Form 24 Financial Institution Bond

Extending credit based on electronic transactions will increase the potential of loan losses due to discovered forgeries.[2] Financial institutions may attempt to bring loan loss claims under Insuring Agreement (E).[3]

---

2. Iga W. Todd, *et al.*, *Enforceable Electronic Signatures Versus Unenforceable Electronic Communication*, *in* THE FIDELITY LAW JOURNAL 177, 227 (Michael Keeley et al. eds., The Fidelity Law Association, Vol. XXIX, Oct. 2023).
3. 1986 FINANCIAL INSTITUTION BOND, Insuring Agreement (E).

Insuring Agreement (E) covers losses resulting from extending credit on the faith of an original of certain enumerated documents. Financial Institution Bonds, however, do not provide blanket coverage for all forgery-related losses.[4] Insuring Agreement (E) covers specific risks, subject to specific elements of coverage.[5] Accordingly, the methodology used by the wrongdoer to perpetrate the fraud and the insured's handling of the underlying transaction will, in many instances, dictate the existence of coverage.[6]

Insuring Agreement (E) codifies the basic premise that Financial Institution Bonds are not "credit insurance."[7] The Bond does not "protect [an insured] when it simply makes a bad business deal."[8] "The failure to follow sound business practices and verify the authenticity is a business risk taken by [the insured] and not an insured risk covered by the Bond."[9] Insuring Agreement (E) requires the insured to comply with minimum banking standards (to ensure that the insurer is not forced to provide coverage for avoidable losses). The "requirement that the bank possess original documents recognizes that the bank is often in the best position to protect itself from a borrower's fraud."[10]

While possession of the original may appear to be a technicality, Financial Institution Bonds impose that basic level of due diligence because a financial institution cannot viably evaluate the existence of a forgery or alteration without inspecting the original document. Courts

---

4. *Enforceable Electronic Signatures Versus Unenforceable Electronic Communication*, *supra* note 2 at 227.
5. *Id.*
6. *Id.*
7. *Enforceable Electronic Signatures Versus Unenforceable Electronic Communication*, *supra* note 2 at 227; Liberty Nat'l Bank v. Aetna, 568 F. Supp. 860, 866 (D.N.J. 1983).
8. *Enforceable Electronic Signatures Versus Unenforceable Electronic Communication*, *supra* note 2 at 227; Republic Nat'l Bank v. Fid. & Guar. Co., 894 F.2d 1255, 1263 (11th Cir. 1990).
9. *Enforceable Electronic Signatures Versus Unenforceable Electronic Communication*, *supra* note 2 at 227-28; Nat'l City Bank v. St. Paul, 447 N.W.2d 171, 177 (Minn. 1989); 9A J. Appleman & J. Appleman, INSURANCE LAW AND PRACTICE § 5701, at 380 (1981) (a bond "does not insure good management nor against the risk of loss inherent in the banking operations: "punctuation").
10. BancInsure, Inc. v. Marshall Bank, N.A., 453 F.3d 1073, 1076 n.2 (8th Cir. 2006).

enforce the original requirement—denying coverage where an insured does not secure the original documents prior to extending credit.[11]

The bond covers transactions involving specifically enumerated documents bearing a qualifying impairment, but only if the insured applies traditional banking practices and obtains the original loan documents before extending credit.[12] Prior to 2004, the bond did not define the term original. Insuring Agreement (E) limits coverage to:

> (E) Loss resulting directly from the Insured having, in good faith, for its own account or for the account of others,
>
> (1) acquired, sold or delivered, or given value, extended credit or assumed liability, on the faith of, any original
>
> (a) Certificated Security,
> (b) Document of Title,
> (c) deed, mortgage or other instrument conveying title to, or creating or discharging a lien upon, real property,
> (d) Certificate of Origin or Title,
> (e) Evidence of Debt,
> (f) corporate, partnership or personal Guarantee,
> (g) Security Agreement,
> (h) Instruction to a Federal Reserve Bank of the United States, or
> (i) Statement of Uncertificated Security of any Federal Reserve Bank of the United States
>
> which
>
> (i) bears a signature of any maker, drawer, issuer, endorser, assignor, lessee, transfer agent, registrar, acceptor, surety, guarantor, or of any person signing in any other capacity which is a Forgery, or
> (ii) is altered, or
> (iii) is lost or stolen;

---

11. Bank of Bozeman v. BancInsure, No. 09–36088, 404 Fed. Appx. 117, 118-19 (9th Cir. 2010); *BancInsure, Inc.*, 453 F.3d at 1075-76; Reliance v. Capital Bankshares, 912 F.2d 756, 758 (5th Cir. 1990); Valley Cmty. Bank v. Progressive Cas. Ins. Co., 854 F. Supp. 2d 697, 706-07 (N.D. Cal. 2012); First Nat'l Bank v. Hartford Accident & Indem. Co., 295 N.W.2d 425, 429 (Iowa 1980); Nat'l City Bank v. St. Paul, 447 N.W.2d 171, 177 (Minn. 1989); Hamilton v. INA, 557 A.2d 747, 750 (Pa. Super. Ct. 1988).
12. *Enforceable Electronic Signatures Versus Unenforceable Electronic Communication*, *supra* note 2 at 228; 1986 FINANCIAL INSTITUTION BOND, Insuring Agreement (E).

(2) guaranteed in writing or witnessed any signature upon any transfer, assignment, bill of sale, power of attorney, Guarantee, endorsement or any items listed in (a) through (h) above;

(3) acquired, sold or delivered, or given value, extended credit or assumed liability, on the faith of any item listed in (a) through (d) above which is a Counterfeit.

Actual physical possession of the items listed in (a) through (i) above by the Insured, its correspondent bank or other authorized representative, is a condition precedent to the Insured's having relied on the faith of such items.

A mechanically reproduced facsimile signature is treated the same as a handwritten signature.[13]

To establish coverage under Insuring Agreement (E), an insured must show that the loss involved an "original" document. Insureds have attempted to argue that "original" includes electronic documents on the basis that such documents are equivalent to original hardcopy documents. Although the 1986 Bond did not define the term "original," in 2004, the Financial Institution Bond was revised to add the "Written, Original" requirement to clarify that electronic documents are not covered documents.[14]

The 2004 Bond defines "Written" to mean "expressed through letters or marks placed upon paper and visible to the eye."[15] That definition makes clear that covered documents exist only in written form and that electronic documents are not "Written."[16] The 2004 Bond defines "Original" to mean "the first rendering or archetype and does not include photocopies or electronic transmissions even if received and printed."[17] Under this definition, electronic documents uploaded and executed digitally are not an "Original".[18] Applying these definitions, financial

---

13 *Id.*

14. Sur. & Fid. Ass'n of Am., FINANCIAL INSTITUTION BOND, Standard Form No. 24 (Revised April 2004), Insuring Agreement (E); Mark J. Krone et al., *Securities Claims, in* HANDLING FIDELITY BOND CLAIMS 279, 289 (Michael Keeley et al. eds., A.B.A. 3d ed. 2019).

15. Sur. & Fid. Ass'n of Am., FINANCIAL INSTITUTION BOND, Standard Form No. 24 (Revised May 2011), Definitions (v).

16. Automated Lending: Speed Sacrifices Security, *supra* note 191.

17. 2004 FINANCIAL INSTITUTION BOND, Definitions (q); 2011 FINANCIAL INSTITUTION BOND, Definitions (q).

18. Automated Lending: Speed Sacrifices Security, *supra* note 191.

institutions adopting digital lending cannot satisfy the "Written, Original" requirement and any resulting loan loss is not covered under Insuring Agreement (E).[19]

The 2004 Bond was revised to add the Written, Original requirement to Insuring Agreement (D). That insuring agreement was also revised in 2004 to clarify that an "electronic or digital signature" does not qualify for coverage of a forgery and added the requirement of actual physical possession of the original forged document.

> (D) Loss resulting directly from the Insured having, in good faith, paid or transferred any Property in reliance on any Written, Original:
> (1) Negotiable Instrument (except an Evidence of Debt),
> (2) Certificate of Deposit,
> (3) Letter of Credit,
> (4) Withdrawal Order,
> (5) receipt for the withdrawal of Property, or
> (6) instruction or advice directed to the Insured and purportedly signed by a customer of the Insured or by a banking institution
>
> which (a) bears a handwritten signature which is a Forgery; or (b) is altered, but only to the extent the Forgery or alteration causes the loss.
>
> Actual physical possession of the items listed in (1) through (6) above by the Insured is a condition precedent to the Insured's having relied on the items.
>
> A reproduction of a handwritten signature is treated the same as the handwritten signature. An electronic or digital signature is not treated as a reproduction of a handwritten signature.[20]

The 2011 Bond further clarifies that electronic documents are not covered by defining "Original" as "the first rendering or archetype and does not include photocopies or electronic transmissions even if received and printed."[21]

---

19. *Id.*
20. 2004 FINANCIAL INSTITUTION BOND, Insuring Agreement (D).
21. 2011 FINANCIAL INSTITUTION BOND, Insuring Agreement (E).

III.
Claim Examples Evaluating the Original Requirement

This coverage issue typically arises in the context of loan losses. A frequently occurring claim involves a lender disbursing loan funds in reliance on a forged loan document. To determine whether the lender obtained the "original" prior to disbursing funds, the claims professional needs to ask the insured how it received the covered document (e.g., email, fax, overnight mail) and the timing of such receipt. The following claim examples illustrate this issue.

A. Mortgage Lender's Reliance on Emailed Forged Power of Attorney

A mortgage lender sought coverage after it made a loan to a borrower in reliance on a forged signature on a power of attorney used to sign the mortgage. The insured closed and disbursed the loan a week after the bad actor forged the purported borrower's signature on a power of attorney appointing himself as attorney-in-fact with respect to the property and authorizing him to borrow sums of money to purchase the property. At the closing, the bad actor signed the mortgage as the borrower's attorney-in-fact. The mortgage lender disbursed the funds the same day. The mortgage lender indicated that the closing was conducted by a title company.

The insured indicated the title company had possession of the original power of attorney and uploaded a copy of it into the mortgage lender's system prior to the closing. The mortgage lender indicated that its document system showed the power of attorney was uploaded several days before the closing and its underwriter reviewed it before the closing. The title company, however, could not confirm whether the uploaded copy was an original. It could not confirm whether it received the original power of attorney prior to, at, or after the closing. The title company indicated it was possible that it received an emailed copy of the executed power of attorney and uploaded that copy into the mortgage lender's system prior to closing. The fact that the title company did not record the original power of attorney with the deed and mortgage until approximately two months after the closing indicated it was possible that the title company was waiting on the original power of attorney.

While the policy was not a Standard Form 24 Bond, the bond required that the insured relied upon a forgery or alteration of any original enumerated document and required that "there was actual physical possession of the said items by the person closing the Real Estate Loan at the time of the closing." As a condition of coverage, the insured had to prove it relied upon an "original" document. The mortgage lender had to establish that it received the original document and that the closing agent was in possession of the forged original document at the time the loan closed. The insured's failure to obtain actual physical possession of the original document precludes coverage.[22]

The purportedly forged power of attorney submitted in the insured's proof of loss contained a black vertical line on each page indicating the document was copied, scanned, or faxed. Courts have found that photocopies and facsimiles do not constitute original documents.[23]

To investigate this, we inquired about the details of the closing, including who conducted the closing, whether it was in-person, and how the closing agent and the insured received the documents. Because the power of attorney was signed (out-of-state) the same day the title company uploaded it into the insured's system, the document uploaded could not have been an original. The title company received a copy of the power of attorney via email or fax from the purported borrower and uploaded the copy into the mortgage lender's system. The mortgage lender did not establish that it received the original before disbursing the funds, or that its closing agent was in possession of the original at the time the loan closed. While the mortgage was predicated on a forged power of attorney, the policy did not cover the loss because the insured did not establish that the person handling the closing physically possessed the original power of attorney at the time of the closing.

---

22. *Bank of Bozeman*, 404 F. App'x at 118-19; *BancInsure, Inc.*, 453 F.3d at 1075-76; *Fremont Reorganizing Corp. ("Signature")*, 2013 WL 12124105, at *13; *Nat'l City Bank of Minn*, 447 N.W.2d at 175-77, 180; *Hamilton Bank*, 557 A.2d at 750-51; *First Nat'l Bank, Colfax*, 295 N.W.2d at 429-30; *Valley Cmty. Bank*, 854 F. Supp. 2d at 706-07.

23. *Marshall Bank, N.A.*, 453 F.3d at 1075-76 (faxed copies of forged personal guarantees not originals); *Fremont Reorganizing Corp. ("Signature")*, 2013 WL 12124105, at *13 (faxed loan documents, including forged deeds, not originals); *Hamilton Bank*, 557 A.2d at 750-51 (photocopies of forged bills of lading not originals).

B. Financial Institution's Reliance on Emailed Forged Subscription Agreements

Second, a financial institution sought coverage under its financial institution bond on the theory that a purported founder of a private equity fund induced the financial institution to approve a line of credit based upon forged subscription agreements purportedly executed by high profile limited partners. Following preliminary discussions with the financial institution, the founder applied for a large line of credit. Despite the size of the loan, the financial institution did not mandate an in-person meeting with the founder. Instead, it communicated exclusively through phone discussions and email.

While the subscription agreements did not constitute qualifying documents, the financial institution did not possess the original subscription agreements prior to extending credit. Instead, it received the subscription agreements via email. The financial institution's decision to extend credit on the faith of an email and not require the original subscription agreements precluded coverage because the bond expressly mandated possession of the original documents. Courts have denied coverage where an insured does not obtain the original prior to extending credit because the failure to do so prevents a bank from competently evaluating whether the document bears a forgery.[24]

C. Title and Escrow Company's Reliance on Forged Warranty Deeds Shipped Via UPS

Third, a title and escrow company sought coverage after fraudsters impersonating property owners of vacant lots induced it to disburse escrow funds for the closing of both lots to fraudulent bank accounts based on forged warranty deeds purporting to convey title. The title and escrow company served as the escrow agent in the fraudulent sale of the vacant lots. The realtor listed the properties for sale unbeknownst to the true property owners.

Upon receipt of a purchase and sale agreement from the realtor, the title and escrow company verified the information with the sellers and

---

24. *E.g.*, *Bank of Bozeman v. BancInsure*, 404 Fed. Appx. at 118-19; *BancInsure, Inc.*, 453 F.3d at 1075-76; *Valley Cmty. Bank*, 854 F. Supp.2d at 706-07.

prepared and emailed the purported owners the statutory warranty deed, amongst other documents, and a UPS label to return the executed documents. The title and escrow company claims the fraudsters forged the warranty deed and filled out the instruction of proceeds form to include their bank information for the receipt of sale proceeds. The title and escrow company wire transferred the sale proceeds from its account to the fraudulent bank account.

To establish coverage under Insuring Agreement (E), the insured had to prove that it paid value or extended credit "on the faith of" any original defective document. While the title and escrow company did not extend credit, it did transfer funds on the faith of the statutory warranty deeds. Insuring Agreement (E) required that the forged document on which the insured relied was an "original" document and the insured had "actual physical possession" of the document. The fraudsters forged the statutory warranty deeds and shipped the deeds to the title and escrow company via UPS. Because the fraudsters shipped the deeds via UPS, the title and escrow company physically possessed the original statutory warranty deeds.

D. Financial Institution's Reliance on Printout of a Fabricated Brokerage Account Statement

Fourth, a financial institution sought coverage after it extended credit based on a fabricated brokerage account statement. The borrower provided account statements for a brokerage account that it pledged to the bank as security for the loan. The account statements were fraudulent fabrications, and the borrower did not own the securities. The borrower provided a physical copy of a printout of a brokerage account statement. The copy of the statement was a printout of an online report. While Insuring Agreement (E) did not cover the claimed loss because an account statement is not one of the categories of documents to which the coverage applies and such statements, though fraudulent, were not forged, altered or counterfeit, and the collateral was fictitious/worthless, the bank did not establish that it received the original documents when it funded the loan. The policy's definition of "Original" made it clear that a printout is insufficient to trigger coverage under Insuring Agreement(E) as it defined "Original" as a "first rendering or archetype" and stated that the definition does not include "photocopies or electronic transmissions even if received and printed."

IV.
Potential Challenges and Investigation Into Whether the Loss Involved an Original Covered Document

Insureds may challenge denials of coverage based upon the Uniform Electronic Signatures Act (UETA) because the only court to find coverage absent possession of the original documents predicated its decision on the UETA.[25] In *Transp. Alliance Bank, Inc. v. BancInsure, Inc.*, the insurer denied coverage because the insured extended credit based upon electronic account statements. While agreeing that the insured received electronic account statements, the district court nonetheless found coverage because the bond did not define the word original and the electronic account statements were originals under the Uniform Electronic Transactions Act (UETA):

> . . . [T]he electronic account statements should be deemed originals based on Utah's Uniform Electronic Transactions Act ("UETA"), which applies to "transactions between parties each of which has agreed to conduct transactions by electronic means," with the parties' intent to be determined by "the context and surrounding circumstances." Utah Code Ann. § 46–4–105(2)(A). Arrow and TAB intended to transact through electronic means when Arrow gave TAB access to its computer system. UETA therefore provides that "[a] record . . . may not be denied legal effect or enforceability solely because it is in electronic form." Utah Code Ann. § 46–4–201(1). UETA also authoritatively states that an electronic document is equivalent to an original document for retention and presentation purposes. Id. at § 46–4–301(4). Not only does UETA demonstrate that the banking world widely recognizes the reality and enforceability of electronic transmissions, but in the last decade several other federal acts have granted legal validity to electronic documents.

Transp. Alliance involved the transmission of electronic account statements—namely electronic information created electronically and communicated through electronic means. The electronic document was therefore the first archetype and the original. This case is distinguishable from most claims which involve hand-signed documents, scanned, and then transmitted via email or fax. Scanned copies of hand-signed documents are not an original—even under the UETA.

25. Transp. Alliance Bank, Inc. v. BancInsure, Inc., No. 1:11CV148-DAK-EJF, 2014 WL 684691, *6-7 (D. Utah Feb. 21, 2014).

The UETA does not automatically treat all electronic versions of a document as an original. It contains a specific provision addressing originals: "If a law requires a record to be presented or retained in its original form, or provides consequences if the record is not presented or retained in its original form, that law is satisfied by an electronic record retained in accordance with Subsection (1)." UETA § 12(d). Under this provision, an electronic record is only deemed an original if "retained in accordance with Subsection (1)." That subsection imposes a specific condition—namely that the document be first generated in its final form as an electronic record:

> (a) If a law requires that a record be retained, the requirement is satisfied by retaining an electronic record of the information in the record which:
>
> (1) accurately reflects the information set forth in the record after it was first generated in its final form as an electronic record or otherwise; and
>
> (2) remains accessible for later reference.

A scanned document transmitted via email does not satisfy Subsection (1). *Transp. Alliance* is also distinguishable from claims involving bonds that define the term "original" such as the 2004/2011 Standard Form 24 Financial Institution Bond. The UETA only applies to transactions where the parties have agreed to conduct transactions electronically. Because the UETA would require the insurer and the insured to consent to the foregoing and the 2004/2011 Bond defines "original" as "the first rendering or archetype and does not include photocopies or electronic transmissions even if received and printed", the UETA could not apply to claims involving bonds that contain the foregoing definition of "original."[26]

In order to establish coverage under Insuring Agreement (E), the insured must prove it had actual physical possession of the covered, "Original" document. The claims professional needs to determine whether the insured physically possessed the "Original" document when it funded the loan. The challenge in such cases is often determining what happened with the original—the who, what, when, and where—as coverage will depend upon the facts and circumstances of the claim. The insured may

26. Jase Brown, *What is an Original Under Insuring Agreement (E)?, in* 26 FIDELITY L.J. 57 (Nov. 2020).

claim that it received the original, but it is crucial to pin down the timing as coverage applies only if the insured possessed the original before extending credit.

If an insured relies on an electronic copy received via email or other electronic means to extend credit prior to receiving the original via mail, the insured cannot establish the "Original" requirement. In the context of a mortgage loan, the claims professional needs to inquire about the details of the closing, including who conducted the closing, whether it was in-person, and how the insured received the documents. If the document was recorded with the county clerk, the claims professional should inquire with the clerk to determine if the original was recorded and when. The goal of these questions is to understand whether the insured possessed an original before it parted with the funds. To question the timing of the insured's receipt of the original, the claims professional should ask whether the insured maintains a record of the received document, whether the document contains a timestamp, and whether the insured has any correspondence and/or any other documents substantiating the insured's receipt of such document.[27]

V.
Conclusion

With the continued digitization of the lending process and reliance on electronic documents, insureds and insurers will grapple with what constitutes an original in the electronic world. Despite society's growing reliance on email and other electronic communications, insurers must require financial institutions to obtain and rely on original documents to prevent fraud and potential claims of forgery. Without this requirement, financial institutions cannot viably evaluate the existence of a covered defect. Claims professionals must pay close attention to the facts and circumstances of claims under Insuring Agreements D) and (E) to evaluate whether the insured had possession of the original when disbursing funds.

---

27. Mark J. Krone et al., *Securities Claims, in* HANDLING FIDELITY BOND CLAIMS 279, 295-96 (Michael Keeley et al. eds., A.B.A. 3d ed. 2019).

CHAPTER 3

COMPUTER FRAUD: AN OLD COVERAGE—NOW IN THE SPOTLIGHT

Carol Z. Smith*

I. Introduction

The threat that computer fraud coverage was designed to insure is a direct attack on a computer system that sends money outside of the business or bank. However, given the increase in technological developments, losses which involve some use of a computer to conduct business transactions have taken on a variety of forms and dramatically increased. What was once an environment in which few computer fraud claims were asserted has changed to an environment in which insurers are frequently asked to consider computer fraud coverage where no direct attack occurred.

This chapter briefly discusses some of the cases in which courts have wrestled with the issue of whether computer fraud coverage is limited to "hacking" or extends to losses sustained as a direct result of social engineering schemes. More importantly, this chapter outlines the common types of attacks being perpetrated against computer systems, what can be done to protect individuals and companies from such attacks, and what to do if you are a victim of a direct attack.

* The author acknowledges the contributions of Nick Espinosa, whose many articles on Cybersecurity are relied upon and cited throughout this chapter. The author also thanks Toni Scott Reed of Clark Hill and Erica Garrett of Dysart Taylor McMonigle Brumitt & Wilcox, P.C. for their contributions.

II.
Background of Computer Fraud Insurance Coverage

Since the 1980s, the insurance industry has offered computer fraud coverage. The ISO Computer Fraud Coverage Form was first sold in 1983 and generally required the insured to prove an unauthorized fraudulent entry of data or change to data in a computer system which caused money to be paid or delivered outside the insured's premises.[1] With respect to the Financial Institution Bond, a rider providing coverage for Computer Systems Fraud was introduced in 1993 for use with the 1986 Edition of the Form 24 Financial Institution Bond. The Rider was designed to provide coverage for the fraudulent entry of data in the insured's computer system that caused property to be transferred or an account at the insured bank to be debited or credited.[2] Both coverages were intended to be limited to hacking incidents.

With the advance of social engineering schemes,[3] insurers were faced with claims that arose from alleged "use" of the insured's computer system in a business transaction, but that did not involve a direct attack on the insured's computer system coupled with a fraudulent transfer. In the face of increasing claims, cases in which the courts interpreted the computer fraud coverage more broadly than intended, and the challenge of appropriately pricing the increased risk, insurers endeavored to redefine and delineate what constitutes computer fraud, as opposed to fraud perpetrated with or incidentally involving the use of a computer, including

---

1. Scott L. Schmookler, *Computer and Funds Transfer Fraud* in COMMERCIAL CRIME INSURANCE COVERAGE, 298-99 (Randall I. Marmor and Susan Koehler Sullivan eds., 2014).
2. Edward G. Gallagaher, *A Concise History of Standard Form No. 24, 1986 ed. in* ANNOTATED FINANCIAL INSTITUTION BOND, 13 (Michael Keeley ed., 2d ed. 2004).
3. Social engineering has been defined as "an umbrella term that describes a variety of cyberattacks that use psychological tactics to manipulate people into taking a desired action." Bart Lenaerts-Bergmans, *Social Engineering Explained*, CROWDSTRIKE CYBERSECURITY 101 THE FUNDAMENTALS OF CYBERSECURITY (May 22, 2023), https://www.crowdstrike.com/en-us/cybersecurity-101/social-engineering/. Common warning signs of a social engineering attack include communications which create a sense of urgency, require time-sensitive responses, request sensitive information via email, or are sent from a similar looking but incorrect email address. *Id.*

social engineering where the fraudster tricks an authorized user of the computer system to themselves transfer money or property. Additionally, insurers now offer specific coverage for social engineering losses, although typically with lower coverage limits.[4] Through these changes and the addition of insuring agreements, insurers attempted to confine losses to the insuring agreement specifically created to cover the particular hazard.

III.
What is "Computer Fraud"?

A typical computer fraud coverage is now written as:

> Computer Fraud. The insurer will pay the *Insured Entity* for its direct loss of *Money, Securities, or Other Property,* directly caused by *Computer Fraud* that is *Discovered* during the Policy Period.
>
> *Computer Fraud*
>
> 1. Means an intentional, unauthorized, and fraudulent entry or change of data or computer instructions, directly into or within, a *Computer System*, that:
>
>   a. is not made by an *Insured Person*, an *Independent Contractor*, or any other person under the direct supervision of the *Insured*; and
>
>   b. causes *Money, Securities, or Other Property* to be transferred, paid or delivered from inside the *Insured Entity's* premises or the *Insured Entity's* financial institution premises to a place outside of such premises.
>
> 2. Does not include *Social Engineering Fraud.*

---

4. For a comprehensive summary of the case law addressing computer fraud and social engineering fraud coverage, *see* J. Caralisa Connell, Justin D. Wear and Michael V. Branley, *Computer Fraud Insuring Agreement and Social Engineering Fraud Insuring Agreement in* THE FINANCIAL INSTITUTION BOND AND COMMERCIAL CRIME POLICY: PRINCIPLES AND ANNOTATIONS (Michael Keeley, Toni Scott Reed, Robert M. Flowers, Megan M. Manogue, and J. Caralisa Connell eds., 2023).

As the above definition shows, in the fidelity/crime insurance context, insurers have endeavored to define "computer fraud" as essentially gaining unauthorized access to data, devices, systems, or networks through a direct attack coupled with a fraudulent transfer. This type of attack typically is achieved by exploiting weaknesses in software and hardware. Insurers have distinguished this type of direct attack against a computer system from a social engineering scheme, where the fraudster manipulates a human being into taking action to make a transfer. In carrying out the latter, the fraudsters shift "their focus away from pure technological attacks and have increasingly attacked employees through the use of 'social engineering'—a collection of techniques used to manipulate people into performing actions or divulging confidential information."[5]

Some courts were persuaded that computer fraud coverage required direct attacks on the insured's computer system and concluded there was no coverage in the absence of hacking. For example, in *Taylor & Lieberman v. Federal Insurance Co.*,[6] the court concluded there was no computer fraud coverage for loss arising from emailed fraudulent directions instructing the insured to wire money to the fraudster's account. The computer fraud coverage required an unauthorized "entry into" the insured's computer system. The court concluded that the fraudster's emails containing the fraudulent directions were not an introduction of instructions that propagated themselves through the computer system.[7]

However, during the evolution of the computer fraud coverage language and applicable exclusions, the courts did not uniformly conclude the policy language sufficiently delineated the difference between computer fraud and social engineering. For example, in *American Tooling Center, Inc. v. Travelers Casualty and Surety Co. of America*,[8] the court concluded there was computer fraud coverage for losses resulting from the insured's wiring money to the fraudster, who was impersonating its vendor, in accordance with fraudulent email instructions.

The policy provided, "[t]he Company will pay the **Insured** for the **Insured's** direct loss of, or direct loss from damage to, **Money, Securities and Other Property** directly caused by **Computer Fraud,**" and defined

---

5. Scott L. Schmookler and Christopher M. Kahler, *Social Engineering: Is the Manipulation of Humans a Computer Fraud?*, 22 FID. L. J. 1, 4 (2016)
6. Taylor & Lieberman v. Fed. Ins. Co., 681 Fed. Appx. 627 (9th Cir. 2017).
7. *Id.* at 629.
8. Am. Tooling Ctr., Inc. v. Travelers Cas. & Sur. Co. of Am., 895 F. 3d 455 (6th Cir. 2018).

Computer Fraud as, "The use of any computer to fraudulently cause a transfer of **Money, Securities or Other Property** from inside the **Premises or Financial Institution Premises**: 1. to a person . . . outside the **Premises or Financial Institution Premises**; or 2. to a place outside the **Premises or Financial Institution Premises**." The court reasoned that the impersonator sent the insured fraudulent emails using a computer and the emails fraudulently caused the insured to transfer the money.[9] The court rejected the insurer's argument that the coverage was limited to "computer hacking" or required the fraudster to gain access to and control the computer, and concluded there was no language in the policy requiring the fraud to cause the computer to cause to transfer the funds.[10]

Likewise, in *Ernst & Haas MGMT. Co., Inc. v. Hiscox,*[11] the court concluded a social engineering scheme resulting in the insured's accounts-payable clerk making payments after receiving fraudulent emails was covered under the computer fraud insuring agreement. The policy covered loss "resulting directly from the use of any computer to fraudulently cause a transfer of that property . . . ." The Ninth Circuit found the district court had erred in construing that language to apply to only loss resulting directly from the unauthorized use of the insured's computers.[12] The court relied heavily on the *American Tooling* decision, which it found to be persuasive.[13]

Another court followed suit in *City of Unalaska v. Nat'l Union Fire Ins. Co.*[14] and concluded that loss resulting from a social engineering scheme involving emailed instructions from a fraudster posing as a vendor constituted computer fraud within the meaning of the policy. The policy's computer fraud insuring agreement stated:

> [Insurer] will pay for loss of or damage to "money," "securities" and "other property" resulting directly from the use of any computer to fraudulently cause a transfer of that property from inside the "premises" or "banking premises" . . . [t]o a person (other than a "messenger")

---

9. *Id.* at 461-62.
10. *Id.* at 462.
11. Ernst & Haas Mgmt. Co. v. Hiscox, Inc., 23 F.4th 1195 (9th Cir. 2022).
12. *Id.* at 1201.
13. *Id.* at 1201-02.
14. City of Unalaska v. Nat'l Union Fire Ins. Co., 591 F. Supp.3d 440 (D. Alaska 2022).

> outside those "premises" [] or . . . [t]o a place outside those "premises."[15]

The insurer argued that the computer fraud insuring agreement only covered computer hacking and incidents involving things like the introduction of malicious computer code rather than losses related to the incidental use of a computer as the means of fraudulent communication.[16] The court disagreed, noting that "a reasonable layperson would consider the phrase 'use of any computer' to encompass a broad range of activities, including sending emails, rather than being limited to instances of computer hacking."[17]

The narrowing of the computer fraud policy language and the availability of social engineering coverage has led to better results for insurers. For example, in *Mississippi Silicon Holdings, LLC v. Axis Insurance Co.*,[18] a case involving a fraudster impersonating a vendor instructing the insured to make payments to another account, the insurer concluded that the loss was covered under the social engineering coverage and paid the applicable limit of that coverage but denied the claim under the computer transfer fraud and funds transfer fraud coverages, which each had higher limits. The policy specifically defined "computer transfer fraud" as "the fraudulent entry of information into or the fraudulent alteration of any information within a Computer System."[19] The court agreed with the insurer that the computer transfer fraud coverage did not exist because nothing entered into or altered the insured's computer system, directly causing the transfer of any money.[20] Rather, it was the insured's own actions which led to the loss. The court additionally found that the availability of coverage for social engineering fraud for the very incident that occurred supported its decision that the computer transfer fraud coverage did not apply.[21]

---

15. *Id.* at 443.
16. *Id.* at 445.
17. *Id.* at 451.
18. Miss. Silicon Holdings, LLC v. Axis Ins. Co., 440 F.Supp.3d 575 (N.D. Miss. 2020).
19. *Id.* at 581.
20. *Id.* at 582.
21. *Id.* at 584.

Likewise in *SJ Computers v. Travelers Casualty & Surety Co. of America*,[22] another case involving a fraudster posing as an existing vendor, the insurer concluded that the loss was covered under the social engineering coverage and paid the applicable limits of that coverage but denied coverage under the computer fraud provision of the policy. The policy defined computer fraud as "an intentional, unauthorized, and fraudulent entry or change of data or computer instructions directly into a **Computer System**," and further provided computer fraud did not include **"Social Engineering Fraud."**[23] The court found that the fraudulent scheme fell precisely within the coverage for social engineering fraud, which covered "the intentional misleading of an **Employee** or **Authorized Person** by a natural person impersonating a . . . **Vendor** . . . through the use of a **Communication**,"[24] and thus could not qualify as computer fraud. Further, addressing the "direct loss" issue, the court rejected the argument that the fraudster's hacking and use of the purchasing manager's email account to send the fraudulent invoices that were paid directly caused the loss.

IV.
How Do Attackers Gain Entry Into Computer Systems?

The discussion above addresses what insurance coverage may be available in the market for computer fraud, how the coverage has evolved, how courts have interpreted the coverage, and how computer fraud is a different hazard than social engineering. The distinctions between computer fraud and social engineering make clear that the insured and the insurer need to understand precisely what actually happened within the insured's computer system (if anything). Thus, when faced with a particular claim, how do you determine what actually happened in the insured's computer system? Specifically, did an attacker gain intentional, unauthorized, and fraudulent access to a computer system, and if so, how?

Although new criminal schemes are being developed daily, the most common ways attackers gain entry into computer systems are phishing, exploiting software vulnerabilities, brute force and credential stuffing attacks, infecting the computer system with malware, Man-in-the-Middle

---

22. SJ Computs., LLC v. Travelers Cas. & Sur. Co. of Am., 621 F. Supp. 3d 962 (D. Minn. 2022).
23. *Id.* at 965.
24. *Id.* at 969.

(MitM) attacks, injection attacks, zero-day exploits, and privilege escalation. Each type of attack is briefly described below.

A. Phishing Attacks

Phishing attacks are a low cost and highly successful way for attackers to gain access to personal data and computer systems. Phishing consists of attackers posing as a legitimate individual or company to steal sensitive information such as usernames, passwords, and other personal details that can give that attacker access into a computer system. The attacker typically uses deceptive emails, text messages, or phone calls that appear to come from a trusted source. The attacker's goal is to trick the user into taking specific action such as clicking on a link, downloading a file, or sharing confidential information. The attacker generally attempts to create a sense of urgency, fear, or curiosity to encourage the user to act quickly without verifying the authenticity of the request.[25]

B. Software Vulnerabilities

Software is not perfect and there are weaknesses that can be exploited by attackers. The Common Vulnerability Scoring System (CVSS) is a free industry standard that cybersecurity organizations use to assess and communicate the severity and characteristics of software vulnerabilities. Typically, a company's security team will use a vulnerability management tool to detect vulnerabilities so they can be patched or remedied as directed by the software developer.[26]

C. Brute Force and Credential Stuffing Attacks

A brute force attack involves the attacker using a trial-and-error approach to systematically guess login information, credentials, and

---

25. Bart Lenaerts-Bergmans, *Introduction to Phishing*, CROWDSTRIKE CYBERSECURITY 101: THE FUNDAMENTALS OF CYBERSECURITY (Oct. 24, 2024), https://www.crowdstrike.com/en-us/cybersecurity-101/social-engineering/phishing-attack/.
26. Bei Wang, *Vulnerability Management*, CROWDSTRIKE CYBERSECURITY 101: THE FUNDAMENTALS OF CYBERSECURITY (Apr. 15, 2023), https://www.crowdstrike.com/en-us/cybersecurity-101/exposure-management/vulnerability-management/.

encryption keys. The attacker repeatedly submits combinations of usernames and passwords in an effort to arrive at the accurate one. In a credential stuffing attack the attacker uses searches with stolen login combinations available to attackers on the dark web. Credential stuffing attacks are successful because many people use the same login names and passwords on several accounts.[27]

D. Malware or Trojans

Malware (malicious software) describes a program or code created to harm a computer, network or server. The attacker introduces malware into the computer system for a variety of reasons, including to extort money from the victim, sabotage the company, steal confidential data, or simply make a statement. There are several types of malware. A Trojan is malware that appears to be legitimate (often free) software to be downloaded on the computer system. Trojans are typically installed through techniques such as phishing or bait websites. Signs that a computer system may have a malware infection include slow computer performance, frequent ads and pop-ups, the battery draining rapidly, system crashes, sudden loss in disk space, browser settings changing on their own, the antivirus product is disabled, lost access to files or the computer, and deleted files.

E. MitM Attacks

A man-in-the-middle (MITM) attack occurs when the attacker eavesdrops on a conversation between two targets and collects personal data, passwords or other sensitive information or convinces the target to take an action such as changing their login credentials or transferring funds. A common point of access for attackers is through messaging services, file storage systems or remote work applications. The attacker may also gain access to a network through an open or poorly secured Wi-Fi router and or by manipulating the domain name system servers. The attacker then tricks users to provide personal information or take certain actions by such ploys as imitating an established internet protocol,

---

27. Bart Lenaerts-Bergmans, *What is Privilege Escalation?*, CROWDSTRIKE CYBERSECURITY 101: THE FUNDAMENTALS OF CYBERSECURITY (June 2, 2022), https://www.crowdstrike.com/en-us/cybersecurity-101/cyber attacks/privilege-escalation/.

redirecting users to a fake website, simulating a Wi-Fi access point, or creating illegitimate secure sockets layer (SSL) certificates to give the appearance of a secure connection when the connection has been compromised.[28]

F. Injection Attacks

An injection attack occurs when an attacker exploits vulnerabilities in a web application, database, operating system, software application and or web server to send malicious code into a system. This type of attack, when successful, allows the attacker to execute unauthorized commands, access data and manipulate the computer system's operation.[29]

G. Zero-Day Exploits

The term "Zero-Day" refers to the situation when security teams are unaware of the company's software vulnerability and they have had zero days to work on a security patch or update to fix the issue. In this context, the attacker releases malware to exploit the software vulnerability before the software developer has patched the flaw.[30]

H. Privilege Escalation

A privilege escalation attack involves the attacker exploiting human behaviors, design flaws or oversights in operating systems or web applications to move deeper into a network to search for high-value assets resulting in an internal or external user having unauthorized system privileges. This type of attack typically starts with a social engineering

---

28. Kurt Baker, *What is a Man in the Middle (MITM) Attack?*, CROWDSTRIKE CYBERSECURITY 101: THE FUNDAMENTALS OF CYBERSECURITY (Jan. 17, 2025), https://www.crowdstrike.com/en-us/cybersecurity-101/cyber attacks/man-in-the-middle-mitm-attack/.
29. Bart Lenaerts-Bergmans, *Injection Attacks*, CROWDSTRIKE CYBERSECURITY 101: THE FUNDAMENTALS OF CYBERSECURITY (May 3, 2024), https://www. crowdstrike.com/en-us/cybersecurity-101/cyber attacks/ injection-attack/.
30. Venu Shastri, *What is a Zero-Day Exploit?*, CROWDSTRIKE CYBERSECURITY 101: THE FUNDAMENTALS OF CYBERSECURITY (Jan. 17, 2025), https://www.crowdstrike.com/en-us/cybersecurity-101/ cyberattacks/zero-day-exploit/.

technique, often an electronic communication that contains a harmful link to compromise a user's account, which then leaves the entire network exposed. Once that happens, the attacker can take a number of actions ranging from sending unauthorized emails to launching malware to a ransomware attack.[31]

V.
What Can Be Done to Prevent or Discourage Direct Attacks?

A. "Defense-in-Depth"

"Defense-in-Depth" refers to a proactive layering of security features on top of each other to protect companies from cyberattacks. This is especially important as companies move to cloud-based processes and employees use mobile devices to check emails and log into company systems to work remotely.[32] The focus of the defense in depth is prevention, detection and response.

1. Patching/Updating Systems

Computer systems are patched and updated for two reasons. First, the updated software may have new features or adjustments to make it perform better or faster. But systems are also updated to address and correct vulnerabilities that have been discovered. Failure to timely install patches and updates leads to increased vulnerability to hackers.[33]

---

31. Bart Lenaerts-Bergmans, *Brute Force Attacks*, CROWDSTRIKE CYBERSECURITY 101: THE FUNDAMENTALS OF CYBERSECURITY (June 1, 2022), https: // www.crowdstrike.com/en-us/cybersecurity-101/cyber attacks/brute-force-attack/.
32. Brett Shaw, *What Is Defense In Depth?*, CROWDSTRIKE CYBERSECURITY 101: THE FUNDAMENTALS OF CYBERSECURITY (Mar. 22, 2022), https://www.crowdstrike.com/en-us/cybersecurity-101/exposure-management/defense-in-depth/.
33. Nick Espinosa, *Can U.S. Cyberdefense Withstand Another Government Shutdown?*, Forbes Technology Council (Feb. 25, 2019), https://www.forbes.com/councils/forbestechcouncil/2019/02/25/can-u-s-cyberdefense-withstand-another-government-shutdown/.

2. *Solid Password and MFA Policies*

Gaining credentials to a computer system allows hackers to impersonate the account owner and appear to be an authorized user. Protection begins with utilizing complex passwords, changing passwords on a periodic basis, and not using the same password for all accounts.

Multi-factor authentication (MFA) is a multi-layered security access management process, which allows users access to a computer system or network only after confirming their identity with one or more credential or authentication factor. MFA procedures involve having unique identifiers each stored in different databases and infrastructures so no single compromised system would allow hackers to gain access to a complete identity. Thus, if the primary authentication factor is compromised or disabled, access is denied unless the user also has control over the secondary authorization factor. This process typically involves use of a combination of a username and a password (something an authorized user knows) and a verification code or one-time password delivered via text or email (something the authorized user has), and/or a biometric identifier (something the authorized user is).[34]

3. *Role Based User Training For Phishing And Proper Hygiene*

Given the proliferation and success of phishing schemes, companies should provide phishing attack awareness training. Training can cover such subjects as typical phishing attacks, commonly used techniques, typical characteristics of phishing messages, the consequences of complying with a phishing message and how to report phishing attempts. Several firms offer training videos that can be effective in alerting and reminding employees of the types of scams and the danger of falling for one.[35]

---

34. Narendran Vaidesswaran, *Multi-Factor Authentication (MFA)*, CROWDSTRIKE CYBERSECURITY 101 THE FUNDAMENTALS OF CYBERSECURITY (Jan. 8, 2025), https://www.crowdstrike.com/en-us/cybersecurity-101/identity-protection/multifactor-authentication-mfa/.
35. Kurt Baker, *How to Implement Phishing Attack Awareness Training*, CROWDSTRIKE CYBERSECURITY 101: THE FUNDAMENTALS OF CYBERSECURITY (Feb. 12, 2023), https://www.crowdstrike.com/en-us/cybersecurity-101/social-engineering/phishing-attack-awareness-training/.

Good individual IT hygiene includes such things as creating strong passwords and protecting them from disclosure; connecting to the network through secure Wi-Fi; being on alert for unsolicited emails or texts with suspicious links; and alerting IT about suspicious activity or accidental breaches. To prevent malware attacks, users should not download software from unknown sources, should refrain from clicking on popups, and should delete apps and programs no longer being used.

4. Technical Security Controls Such As Endpoint Threat Detection / Perimeter Threat Detection / Network Detection and Response

Endpoint security or protection relates to defending user endpoints—any device that connects to the company network from outside its firewall. Endpoints include laptops, tablets, point-of-sale (POS) systems, digital printers, and mobile devices from attacks. Endpoint protection systems work by examining files, processes, and system activity for evidence of suspicious or malicious activities.[36]

5. Applying the Principle of Least Privilege

The principle of least privilege (POLP) is a computer security concept that gives users limited access rights based on the tasks necessary to their job. It is a practice designed to strengthen an organization's cyber security by controlling and monitoring network and data access. This is accomplished by the system administrator attributing privileged access to user accounts according to that portion of the system to which the user needs access. This limits, and thus protects, access to the accounts of the administrator(s) of the system, those who need a high level of access to perform network monitoring and maintenance.[37]

---

36. Anne Aarness, *EndPoint Security: How Endpoint Protection Works*, CROWDSTRIKE CYBERSECURITY 101: THE FUNDAMENTALS OF CYBERSECURITY (Jan. 7, 2025), https://www.crowdstrike.com/en-us/cybersecurity-101/endpoint-security/.
37. Narendran Vaidesswaran, *Data Encryption Explained*, CROWDSTRIKE CYBERSECURITY 101: THE FUNDAMENTALS OF CYBERSECURITY (May 10, 2023), https://www.crowdstrike.com/en-us/cybersecurity-101/data-protection/ data-encryption/.

6. Encryption of Sensitive Data and Internet/Network Traffic

Data encryption ensures that data cannot be read, stolen, or altered while stored or in transit. Data encryption converts plain text into an encoded format to protect against unauthorized access to data and to maintain confidentiality of the protected information.[38]

7. Building Proper Incident Response Plans for Various Scenarios

Having an incident response plan before the need for a response to a cyberattack is a key component to minimizing the impact of the event. The National Institute of Standards and Technology (NIST) promulgated an incident response plan with the following steps: (1) preparation; (2) detection and analysis; (3) containment, eradication and recovery; and (4) post-incident activity.[39]

The preparation phase involves putting together the team, tools and processes likely to be needed before an incident occurs. The detection and analysis phase refers to identifying the security incident, determining its scope, and analyzing its characteristics. The containment, eradication and recovery phase entails isolating the threat, removing it from the computer system, and restoring normal operations. Post-incident activity relates to learning from the incident to improve future preparedness.[40]

VI.
What Do You Do If Your Computer System is Hacked?

In the event your computer system is hacked, the first thing to do is not panic. There are steps that need to be taken as soon as practicable to restore functionality to the computer system and protect against additional loss. There are also lessons to be learned to improve security in the future.

---

38. Vaidesswaran, *Multi-Factor Authentication (MFA)*, *supra*.
39. JJ Cranford, *Incident Response Plan: Frameworks and Steps*, CROWDSTRIKE CYBERSECURITY 101: THE FUNDAMENTALS OF CYBERSECURITY (Jul. 6, 2023), https://www.crowdstrike.com/en-us/cybersecurity-101/incident-response/incident-response-steps/.
40. Insane Cyber, *Mastering the Incident Response Process: A Deep Dive into the NIST and SANS Frameworks* (last visited Aug. 16, 2025), https://insanecyber.com/incident-response-frameworks-nist-vs-sans/.

It is imperative to first identify the threat. This will enable an investigation into how the threat occurred and its impact. Once that has occurred, action must be taken to contain the threat. That can include unplugging infected equipment and disconnecting the internet so the infection cannot communicate home. It will then be possible to eradicate the threat, but steps should be taken to preserve any evidence necessary to investigate what occurred.

Once the threat has been resolved, all credentials should be reset and systems can be recovered from backup systems. Communicating with key stakeholders is a sensitive yet necessary step. While no one is excited to disclose a data breach, it is important to disclose what occurred to those involved so they can take proper steps to secure their data to the extent possible.[41] Reporting the incident to authorities should also be contemplated.

VII.
Conclusion

As technology and computer systems advance, so too do the schemes used to perpetrate attacks and fraud. Because only a third party's direct access to an insured's computer system is contemplated by the computer fraud insuring agreement, it is imperative to understand all potential methods of attack that may be used and the strategies for mitigating them.

41. Nick Espinosa, *Betraying Public Trust: When Tech Companies Fail Us*, Forbes Technology Council (Feb. 6, 2018), https://www.forbes.com/sites/forbestechcouncil/2018/02/06/betraying-public-trust-when-tech-companies-fail-us/.

CHAPTER 4

THE BUSINESS COMPUTING ENVIRONMENT—COMPONENTS AND BASIC TECHNOLOGY FOR THE NON-IT PROFESSIONAL

Mark J. Krone
John W. Lippe*

I. Introduction

There is no lack of data showing that computer crime is growing and it shows no sign of leveling off. While cyber policies have evolved to respond to a range of breach types, the ubiquity of digital processing also means that many claims under crime policies arise from fraud actors using computers to execute their schemes. To determine whether coverage applies and under which insuring agreement, it is essential to understand the computer's role in the scheme and the extent to which it impacts the coverage analysis. Easier said than done. While it is tempting to think of the computer simply as the screen on top of your desk, the modern

* This chapter is for general informational purposes only and is not legal advice. It is not designed to be comprehensive, and it may not apply to your particular facts and circumstances. Furthermore, federal, state or local laws, regulations, standards or codes may change from time to time and the audience should always refer to the most current requirements. Consult as needed with your own attorney or other professional advisor. This presentation does not amend, or otherwise affect, the provisions or coverages of any insurance policy. Any discussion of coverages is about those generally available in the marketplace and is not based specifically on the policies or products of any particular carrier.

business computing environment typically consists of numerous separate devices and services.

This chapter will provide a high level introduction to the business computing environment for the non-IT professional. Here, we will identify the common components and services, describe their function and provide some insight into the issues a claims professional could investigate to better understand the relationship between the breached system and the loss.

Because this chapter is intended for professionals analyzing claims under crime policies, not cyber policies, the discussion will be tailored accordingly. As such, the chapter does not dwell on issues that involve privacy breaches, data restoration, regulatory proceedings and the like. Rather, the discussion will focus on issues and analyses that often implicate the common insuring agreements found in crime policies, such as employee theft, computer fraud, funds transfer fraud and social engineering fraud.

II. Modems

A modem connects a computer or a network to the internet by converting digital data from a computer into signals that can be transmitted over telephone lines, cable systems or other types of communication channels. For personal use, a modem is typically a small, standalone device provided by an internet service provider (ISP) that connects a single home or small office network to the internet. It is designed for ease of use and basic functionality, suitable for everyday activities like browsing the web, streaming videos and checking emails. In contrast, an enterprise modem is part of a larger, more complex network infrastructure designed to support the high-speed, reliable internet connectivity needs of a business. In an enterprise-network architecture, the concept of a modem is implemented with a router enabling advanced features such as higher bandwidth capacity, enhanced network protocols and the ability to manage multiple connections simultaneously, ensuring efficient and secure communication across a large organization.

Small business and personal use modems come in several common types, each serving different internet connection needs. The most prevalent types are digital subscriber line (DSL) modems, cable modems and fiber-optic modems. DSL modems use telephone lines to provide internet access and are typically slower than other types, but they are widely available and often sufficient for basic internet activities. Cable modems, on the other hand, use the same coaxial cables that deliver cable television, offering faster speeds than DSL and supporting more bandwidth, making them suitable for streaming and gaming. Fiber-optic modems are the fastest among these options, using light signals through fiber-optic cables to deliver high-speed internet, ideal for heavy internet users and households with multiple devices. While DSL modems are generally more affordable, cable and fiber-optic modems offer superior performance, with fiber-optic modems being the most advanced and reliable for high-demand internet usage.

On the enterprise level, routers are designed to meet the robust internet connectivity needs of businesses and organizations. The most prevalent types include T1 and T3 routers, supporting fiber-optic connectivity with the possibility of cellular modem backup. T1 and T3 routers are traditional options that provide dedicated leased lines for reliable and consistent internet access, often used by businesses requiring stable connections for critical operations. Routers with fiber-optic connectivity are increasingly popular in enterprises due to their ability to deliver high-speed internet with minimal latency, supporting large data transfers and multiple simultaneous connections, which is essential for modern business applications and cloud services. Cellular modems offer flexibility and mobility, enabling internet access through cellular networks, which is particularly useful for remote locations or as a backup connection to ensure business continuity. Each type of enterprise router is tailored to specific business needs, with fiber-optic connectivity generally offering the highest performance and scalability for growing organizations. Most organizations incorporate redundancy in their network router design by having a "hot spare" device ready to take over in case the primary router experiences a hardware failure.

Network firewalls and routers are subject to compromise. Cybercriminals can compromise modems firewalls by exploiting vulnerabilities in the devices' firmware or configuration settings. They often use techniques such as phishing attacks to trick users into revealing login credentials or deploying malware that targets modem software. *This is a significant security risk because the modem serves as the gateway to a business's entire network and connected devices.* Once the hacker gains access, they can alter the modem's settings, redirecting internet traffic to malicious sites or intercepting data being transmitted.[1]

While a compromised modem is not often the direct cause of a loss, a compromised modem may be the entry vector that leads to other computer compromises. If the insured believes that a firewall has been compromised, consider exploring the following:

> Background Information: Has the insured detected unusual activity, such as unexpected changes in internet speed, unauthorized access to accounts or unfamiliar devices connected to the network?
>
> Physical Device: While uncommon, are there physical signs of tampering or unauthorized devices connected to the network?
>
> Compare the firmware to the manufacturer's specs: Is the firewall's firmware up to date? Does the release number match a published firmware release? Does the device contain unknown, open-source software packages?
>
> Analyze the network traffic: Examine network traffic logs to identify unusual patterns or connections to suspicious Internet Protocol (IP) addresses, which may suggest that the firewall is being used for malicious activities.
>
> Review the firewall or router's security settings: Review the configuration and security settings, including password strength and encryption protocols, to ensure they are robust and have not been altered by a hacker.
>
> Perform Threat Analysis: Conduct a thorough review of the open connections and sessions on the firewall and all devices connected to the network to identify any nefarious back door access or malicious software that may have been introduced through the potential network compromise.

Understanding how the scheme was perpetrated and by whom is key to assessing coverage, so the inquiries mentioned above can be crucial. The fact that the insured's connection to the internet shows unusual traffic

---

1. Kevin Parrish, *7 Signs of a Hacked Router and How to Fix It*, HighSpeedInternet.com (Feb. 25, 2025), https://www.highspeedinternet.com/resources/how-to-fix-a-hacked-router.

and anomalous IP addresses, is potential evidence that the claimed loss is not the product of a dishonest employee and supports the possibility of a cybercriminal. The findings can point to further avenues of inquiry to locate how the scheme was carried out.

III. Firewalls

A network firewall device is a critical component in protecting a computer network from unauthorized access and cyber threats. Firewalls monitor incoming and outgoing traffic and decide whether to allow or block specific traffic based on a defined set of security rules.[2] Essentially, it decides which traffic is allowed to pass through and which should be blocked, preventing unauthorized access to the network. Firewalls can be hardware-based, software-based or a combination of both. A hardware firewall is a physical device that sits between the network and the internet, providing robust protection by filtering traffic at the network level. It is often used in enterprise environments for its ability to handle large volumes of traffic and provide additional features like Virtual Private Network (VPN) remote-access support and intrusion detection on the perimeter of the network

Not surprisingly, firewalls can be compromised. Sometimes it is a matter of the hacker exploiting known vulnerabilities, outdated systems, unpatched security flaws or misconfigurations. Alternatively, a cybercriminal might attempt a brute force attack, whereby the hacker systematically keeps inputting different combinations until the correct one is found. Hackers might employ social engineering tactics to trick individuals into revealing login credentials or other sensitive information that can be used to bypass firewall security.

A compromised firewall "opens the door for malware deployment, data theft, lateral movement within the network and even complete network shutdowns. For organizations relying on these firewalls, this could mean business disruption, loss of sensitive data and exposure to regulatory and financial consequences."[3] Once a firewall is compromised,

---

2. Reza Rafati, *Responding to a Potentially Compromised Firewall* (Apr. 25, 2024), https://threatintelligencelab.com/blog/responding-to-a-potentially-compromised-firewall/.
3. Patrick Tiquet, *More Than 2,000 Palo Alto Networks Firewalls Compromised*, Security Magazine (July 9, 2024), https://www.security

hackers can gain access to the internal network, allowing them to intercept data, monitor communications and access sensitive information. Additionally, hackers can redirect network traffic to malicious sites, intercept communications or alter data being transmitted, potentially causing monetary losses.

A traditional firewall only keeps the logs showing activity for a short period of time. It is important for organizations to consider sending the various firewall activity logs to a secure, central location where they can be stored and analyzed as part of a more robust alerting and cyber security operations design.

If a firewall breach is suspected, a professional may consider the following lines of investigation:

> Determine whether activity logs suggest a breach: Are users reporting slow performance? Is the firewall returning security errors or alerts? Are all users known or are there new, unknown accounts?
>
> Review Firewall Logs: Firewall logs should record any suspicious activity, such as repeated failed login attempts, unusual traffic patterns or connections to known malicious IP addresses.
>
> Check Configuration Settings: Verify the firewall's configuration settings to ensure they have not been altered. Look for changes in rules, policies or permissions that could indicate unauthorized access or new, back door connections.

As with modems and other forms of internet connection, this line of inquiry into the firewall is helpful to determine whether there has been an intrusion or whether the alleged compromise is internal. Understanding how a firewall has been breached can help locate the computers that have been compromised.

IV.
Routers

The term "router" refers to networking equipment moving data packets from one computer network to another. Stated in plain English, a router is a device that connects multiple networks and routes data between

---

magazine.com/articles/101209-more-than-2-000-palo-alto-networks-firewalls-compromised.

them. The key concept is that the router works between two networks in order to move communications between them. It is helpful to think of a router as a traffic director and gatekeeper that resides between the business network and the internet.

Routers are susceptible to various forms of cyberattacks if not properly secured. They are attractive targets because they sit at the center of all internet activity within a business network. Hackers may exploit vulnerabilities in the router's firmware or software, especially if it is outdated or improperly configured. They can also use techniques such as brute force attacks to guess weak passwords or employ social engineering tactics to gain access to administrative credentials. By taking control of the router, a cybercriminal can monitor or manipulate all data passing through it, rather than targeting devices one by one. For example, the hacker could silently redirect insurance professionals to fake versions of websites (such as online banking or legal research tools) to steal login credentials, or intercept confidential communications sent over the internet. In some cases, the hacker may install malicious software on the router that gives them ongoing access or turns the router into part of a larger network of infected devices (called a botnet), which can be used to launch attacks on other organizations. Because router compromises often go unnoticed, they provide a stealthy and powerful way to commit cybercrimes, including theft of client data, surveillance and unauthorized access to systems, actions that can have serious legal implications.

When investigating whether a router has been compromised by a hacker, the lines of inquiry are similar to what has been described above.

> Check for any unusual changes in network performance, such as slow internet speeds, frequent disconnections, or unexpected behavior from connected devices. These could be indicators of a compromised router.
>
> Examine the router's logs for any suspicious activity. Look for repeated failed login attempts, unusual traffic patterns or connections to unfamiliar IP addresses. These logs can provide valuable insights into potential breaches.
>
> Verify the router's configuration settings to ensure they have not been altered. Look for changes in security settings, passwords or permissions that could indicate unauthorized access.

Ensure the router's firmware is up to date. Outdated firmware can have vulnerabilities that hackers exploit. Regular updates help protect against known security flaws.

Perform a comprehensive security audit of the router and the network it manages. This may involve using security tools to scan for vulnerabilities and assess the overall security posture.

If necessary, collaborate with IT security experts to perform more advanced diagnostics and forensic analysis. They can help uncover hidden threats or vulnerabilities that may not be immediately apparent.

These types of investigations into the router's status and its traffic history potentially yield insight into whether the compromise is coming from within the insured's ranks or whether there is an outside intrusion.

V. Switches

A network switch is a physical device used within a business to connect multiple computers, printers, servers and other devices on the same internal network so they can communicate with each other efficiently. In a business setting, a switch plays a vital role behind the scenes by directing data only to the device for which it is meant, rather than broadcasting it to every device on the network. This keeps communication fast, organized and secure. For example, when an insurance professional sends a document to the office printer or accesses a shared drive, the switch ensures that data is delivered directly and efficiently. Unlike a router, which connects a business to the internet, the switch works entirely within the local office network, managing internal traffic and ensuring reliable communication between all connected devices. It is especially important in environments with many users or devices, such as an insurance company, where multiple people may be working on different tasks at the same time.

While routers and switches sound similar, they are distinct devices with distinct functions. At a very high level, a router works *between* networks. Typically, a router connects a local network to the internet. A switch works *within* a network, connecting devices to each other.

Although switches are not common targets in comparison to routers or computers, they can be compromised. Common methods of compromising a switch include exploiting default login credentials that were never changed, using outdated firmware with known security flaws or physically accessing the switch in an unsecured location. Other methods involve spoofing the Media Access Control (MAC) address or the Address Resolution Protocol (ARP) of a legitimate device, e.g., a trusted computer, to impersonate the legitimate device and gain unauthorized access to network resources. Once compromised, a hacker can quietly observe internal communications, capture sensitive information like client names, case files or emails, or even disrupt internal systems.

Investigating whether a network switch has been compromised by a hacker requires a combination of observation and system access. Unlike a router, a switch does not usually have obvious signs of compromise, such as internet slowdowns or website redirections. However, the insured may notice unusual internal behavior, including frequent disconnections between computers and printers, delays in accessing shared files or strange network activity during off-hours. Additionally, reviewing the device logs, which record recent activity, such as login attempts, configuration changes or unexpected traffic patterns, is crucial. It is also important to check for unauthorized devices on the network and inspect the switch's settings for signs of tampering, such as altered port configurations or unusual traffic forwarding rules. Another red flag is if the switch is running outdated firmware, which can expose known vulnerabilities. Because most business-grade switches are managed remotely, unauthorized access could also manifest as unexplained remote logins.

VI.
Wireless Access Points

A wireless access point (WAP) is a device that allows computers, smartphones and other wireless devices to connect to a business's internal network without using physical cables. It serves as the bridge between the wired network and wireless users, extending the reach of the network to areas where it would be impractical or inconvenient to run ethernet cables, including conference rooms, reception areas or shared office spaces. In a business setting, wireless access points are essential for enabling secure and reliable Wi-Fi access for staff, guests and mobile devices.[4]

---

4. Cisco Systems, Inc., *What is a Wireless Access Point?*, Cisco (May 2025), https://www.cisco.com/site/us/en/learn/topics/small-business/what-is-an-access-point.html.

A WAP is similar to a network switch in that both allow multiple devices to connect to the same internal network and shared resources, such as printers, files and internet access. Both manage the flow of data within a local network and help ensure that information reaches the right destination. However, they differ in how they connect devices: a switch uses physical cables (ethernet), while a WAP uses radio signals (Wi-Fi). Additionally, switches typically offer faster and more stable connections, making them ideal for devices that stay in one place, like desktop computers or servers. On the other hand, WAPs provide mobility and flexibility, which is increasingly important in modern office environments. Both play complementary roles in a business network, with switches forming the backbone of wired infrastructure and WAPs extending that infrastructure to mobile and portable devices.

WAPs are common targets for hackers, particularly because they provide a potential entry point into a business's internal network without needing physical access to the building. Since WAPs transmit data over the air, they can be detected and attacked from outside the office, sometimes even from a nearby parking lot. Hackers may try to compromise a WAP by exploiting weak or outdated encryption, guessing or stealing Wi-Fi passwords or taking advantage of default settings that were never changed. One common method is a "man-in-the-middle" attack, where the hacker sets up a rogue access point with a similar name to the real network, tricking users into connecting to it. Once connected, the attacker can intercept emails, login credentials or other sensitive data. Another tactic involves exploiting vulnerabilities in the WAP's firmware, especially if it has not been updated, allowing the hacker to gain administrative control of the device. Once a WAP is compromised, a hacker may monitor all wireless activity, spread malware to connected devices or use the WAP as a foothold to move deeper into the business network.

By now, the procedures to investigate whether a cybercriminal has compromised a WAP should feel familiar.

> Confirm who should have access. A WAP's management interface can generate a list of users, devices and configurations. If the insured finds unfamiliar users or devices, that suggests the device has been compromised.
>
> Review the WAP's configuration settings. A compromised WAP may have had its settings altered to give the hacker a backdoor. Thus, it is

helpful to verify whether the default username/passwords have been changed properly and whether the WAP is using the latest software from the manufacturer.

Inspect the physical device. While uncommon, it is worth considering whether the network has been physically breached. That is, a fraud actor might have swapped or added a physical device. If this is a possibility, look for extra or unfamiliar hardware, access points in odd locations and wires leading where they should not.

Review the logs. WAPs keep a log of their activity, which shows who tried to access the system and when. If a breach is suspected, the logs should be reviewed for login attempts at strange hours, IP addresses that do not make sense and repeated failed login attempts. Organizations should consider sending the logs to a secure, central location where longer retention can be established.

A WAP often functions like a hybrid firewall and switch. Thus, a WAP's history logs, authorized users and change history can shed significant light into the nature of a breach and its origin.

VII.
Servers

A server is a hardware device or software that processes requests sent over a network and replies to them. A server functions much like a central filing system, receptionist and traffic controller all rolled into one, only in the digital world. It is a dedicated computer designed to manage, store and distribute data and services to other computers, known as clients, within a network. For example, when employees access shared documents, send emails within the company or use business applications, those actions are often facilitated by a server. It ensures that authorized users can access the resources they need while keeping unauthorized users out.[5] Servers can provide various functionalities, which can include sharing data or resources among multiple clients (i.e., connected computers) or performing computations for a client.

Business enterprise servers are favored targets for cybercriminals due to the critical role they play in storing and managing vast amounts of

5. GeeksforGeeks, *What is a Server?*, GeeksforGeeks (Nov. 17, 2023), https://www.geeksforgeeks.org/computer-networks/what-is-server/.

sensitive and valuable data. These servers often contain confidential business information, customer records, financial data, intellectual property and employee details, making them attractive for data theft and exploitation. Cybercriminals may seek to access this data for various malicious purposes, including identity theft, corporate espionage or selling the information on the dark web. Attackers may use techniques such as ransomware to encrypt data and demand payment for its release, or they may exploit vulnerabilities to gain unauthorized access and control over the server. In the context of a crime policy, a server vulnerability may allow the hacker to add employees to the payroll, change the account information for the insured's payees or create false shipping orders that cause the insured to send its products to the hacker. A compromised server, especially a mail server, may provide the necessary information to allow the cybercriminal to pose as the insured to the insured's bank and cause fraudulent wires to be sent to accounts under the fraud actor's control.

Some common types of servers and their functions are detailed below.

A. Database Servers

These servers maintain and share any form of database over a network. A database is an organized collection of data with predefined properties that may be displayed in a table. Clients of these servers are spreadsheets, accounting software, asset management software or virtually any computer program that consumes well-organized data, especially in large volumes.[6]

Cybercriminals are drawn to database servers because exploiting them can give direct access to vast amounts of confidential data, often with little effort. Common attacks include Structured Query Language (SQL) injection, which allows hackers to manipulate or extract data by inserting malicious commands into application queries. Distributed denial-of-service (DDoS) attacks, buffer overflows and malware are also employed to disrupt access or corrupt data. Many incidents of large-scale breaches arise from improperly secured database servers, particularly those unintentionally exposed to the internet or lacking basic protections such as access controls, encryption and regular patching. For insurance professionals, the stakes are clear: a successful attack on a database server can lead to data leaks, regulatory penalties, legal liability and reputational harm. Vigilant security measures, such as rigorous configuration

6. *Id.*

management, frequent updates, strong authentication and proactive monitoring, are essential to help safeguard these critical systems.[7]

B. Mail Servers

A mail server handles the sending, receiving, and storage of email messages. It manages email accounts, filters spam, and ensures secure communication between users. Mail servers are vital for maintaining effective communication within and outside the organization.

Email is a major vector for phishing, malware and business email compromise attacks. Compromising a mail server offers a high-impact payoff. Through tactics such as spoofing, intercepting or planting malicious attachments, attackers can impersonate trusted colleagues or clients to extract sensitive information or execute fraud. Moreover, vulnerabilities in mail server software, such as the well-documented Exim issue exploited by the Sandworm group, allowed attackers to gain remote access simply by sending a crafted email to the server and then use that foothold to infiltrate the broader network.[8] Exim is a popular and free mail transfer agent used on Unix-like operating systems (such as Linux), that transfers electronic mail messages from one computer to another using the Simple Mail Transfer Protocol.[9] The group known as "Sandworm" are alleged to be a part of the GRU Main Center for Special Technologies (GTsST).[10] The attackers were able to gain root access to Unix-like systems simply by sending a command in the "MAIL FROM" field of the message. From there, Sandworm could add privileged users to the machine, disable network security settings and execute additional scripts

---

7. Lucy Manole, *7 Ways Cybercriminals Exploit Vulnerabilities to Gain Unauthorized Database Access*, IEEE Comput. Soc'y: Tech News (Jul. 2024), https://www.computer.org/publications/tech-news/trends/vulnerabilities-cybercriminals-exploit.
8. Andy Greenberg, *NSA: Russia's Sandworm Hackers Have Hijacked Mail Servers, Wired* (May 28, 2020), https://www.wired.com/story/nsa-sandworm-exim-mail-server-warning/.
9. *See, e.g.*, *Exim*, Wikipedia, https://en.wikipedia.org/wiki/Exim#cite_note-3 (last visited July 22, 2025).
10. Bitdefender, *Russian Sandworm Hackers Attacking Exim Email Servers, Says NSA*, Hot for Security (June 14, 2024), https://www.bitdefender.com/en-us/blog/hotforsecurity/russian-sandworm-hackers-attacking-exim-email-servers-says-nsa/.

for additional exploitation.[11] Once control is obtained, hackers can access historic communications, escalate privileges or distribute malware internally, potentially causing a cascade of damage. With this control, hackers potentially have sufficient information to pose as the insured to its own clients, redirecting client payments to the hackers' account. Potentially, the hackers have amassed enough banking information to pose as the insured's bank and convince the insured to share the token numbers necessary to authorize wire transfers. For insurance professionals, this means a compromised mail server can expose confidential client materials, trigger regulatory breaches and open the door to significant legal or financial liability.

C. Proxy Servers

A proxy server acts as an intermediary between a user's computer and the internet, and in a business environment, it serves multiple important functions, primarily security, control and performance. When someone in the office accesses a website or online service, the request goes through the proxy server first, which then makes the request on the user's behalf. This allows the proxy to filter content, block access to certain websites and monitor internet usage, all of which can help a business enforce internal policies and protect against inappropriate or risky online behavior. It also masks internal IP addresses, which adds a layer of anonymity and protection against external threats. In some cases, proxy servers can cache frequently visited websites, allowing them to load faster for users and reducing internet bandwidth usage.

Reasons to use a proxy server include content control and filtering, improving traffic performance, preventing unauthorized network access and simply routing the traffic over a large and complex network. Careful consideration should be made when using remote desktop services through a proxy server as this is a common target for hackers.

A proxy server is not typically the primary target of cybercriminals in the same way an enterprise server might be, but it can still be of interest depending on how it is configured and used. That is, a proxy server acts as an intermediary between a user's device and the internet, often used to

---

11. National Security Agency, *Sandworm Actors Exploiting Vulnerability in Exim Mail Transfer Agent* (May 28, 2020), https://media.defense.gov/2020/May/28/2002306626/-1/-1/0/CSA-Sandworm-Actors-Exploiting-Vulnerability-in-Exim-Transfer-Agent-20200528.pdf.

filter traffic, hide internal network details or control user access to certain online resources. While it usually does not store sensitive business data, a compromised proxy server can still be valuable to hackers. For example, cybercriminals may exploit an unsecured proxy server to reroute or monitor internet traffic, potentially capturing login credentials or sensitive communications. They may also use it to mask their own identities while launching attacks on other systems, making the business unknowingly complicit. Additionally, if the proxy server is poorly secured, it may provide a pathway into the broader corporate network. For these reasons, while not always a high-value target, proxy servers must still be properly configured and protected to prevent abuse and maintain the integrity of the company's IT environment.

D. Application Servers

An application server runs specific business software (such as case management or billing systems) that users access through their computers. Common applications found on an application server include accounting and finance software, or enterprise resource planning (ERP) systems, which manage billing, payroll and financial reporting. Customer relationship management (CRM) systems are also frequently hosted on application servers to help track interactions with clients or customers, manage sales pipelines and store contact information. Human resources (HR) applications may handle employee records, benefits management and performance tracking. In many offices, project management tools are used to assign tasks, set deadlines and monitor progress across teams. Additionally, document management systems allow for secure storage, retrieval and version control of company documents. By placing these applications on a centralized server, businesses can reduce the need to install and update software on every individual computer, improve data security, support remote access and ensure that employees are always using the most current version of the tools they need.

If an attacker gains control of an application server, they may be able to manipulate how applications behave, extract confidential information or disrupt critical services. Additionally, many application servers are exposed to the internet to allow remote access or customer interaction, which increases the risk of attack if proper security measures are not in place. Vulnerabilities such as unpatched software, weak authentication or poor configuration can give cybercriminals a way in.

While the investigation of a potentially compromised server is complex and typically within the purview of an IT professional, the general procedures are familiar. That is, one would look for unexpected outbound network traffic, which can signal that the server is communicating with a hacker-controlled command-and-control server, often used to transfer stolen data. Similarly, signs of unusual logins, such as access from unfamiliar locations or at odd hours, or privileged account use beyond normal patterns, can indicate someone has obtained unauthorized credentials. On the system itself, strange processes or configuration changes, such as services being enabled, antivirus tools disabled or unknown scheduled tasks installed may indicate malware or active tampering. An examination of log files for odd activity, such as sudden log clearing, unusual error messages or disabled audit trails, might also point to an intrusion.[12]

VIII.
Clients

In a business computing environment, "network client" is a broad term that refers to any computer, device or software application that connects to and uses the resources provided by a server within a network. Clients rely on servers for various functions such as accessing files, sending and receiving emails, using shared printers or authenticating users. Think of the client as a requester of services and the server as the provider. For insurance professionals, this could include everything from a desktop workstation accessing a cloud-based case management system to a mobile device retrieving policy documents from an insurer's intranet.

Network clients can be found in various forms, including personal computers, smartphones, tablets and Internet of Things (IoT) devices. Personal computers, whether desktops or laptops, are common network clients used in both home and business environments to access web services, email and shared files. Smartphones and tablets serve as mobile network clients, enabling users to connect to the internet, use applications and communicate via messaging services. Even printers, if connected to the network, are clients. That is, they have their own IP addresses and can

12. Nat'l Inst. of Standards & Tech., U.S. Dep't of Com., Special Publication 800-61r3 *Incident Response Recommendations and Considerations for Cyber Security Risk Management*, available at https://nvlpubs.nist.gov/nistpubs/SpecialPublications/NIST.SP.800-61r3.pdf.

communicate with other devices on the network. The term "client" is broad enough to encompass IoT devices, such as smart thermostats and security cameras.

While high-end servers may seem like the more obvious target for cybercrime, attackers often begin with client devices because they represent the weakest link in the security chain because they are the devices most employees use to interface with the company network. Though insureds routinely train their staff, employ robust filters and take other reasonable measures, human error is far and away the primary cause of a computer breach.[13] Network client devices that are most frequently targeted by cybercriminals include desktop computers, laptops and smartphones because they often store or have access to confidential client information, financial records and legal documents. Smartphones are particularly attractive in funds transfer fraud because they potentially provide both the necessary data for banking access and allow the phone to be spoofed or cloned so the fraud actor can authenticate a wire transfer request.

Has a client device been compromised? Consider investigating the following:

> Unexpected software changes: Are there new or unfamiliar applications installed on the device or unexpected changes to software configurations?
>
> Disabled security features: Have the antivirus software, firewall or other security features been disabled or have they been uninstalled without the insured's knowledge?
>
> Unusual network activity: Is there evidence of unusual outbound network connections or traffic to unfamiliar destinations?
>
> System performance anomalies: Does the device slow down significantly, freeze, crash or reboot unexpectedly?

---

13. Tony Bradley, *The Human Factor: Redefining Cybersecurity in the Age of AI*, Forbes (Mar. 21, 2025), https://www.forbes.com/sites/tonybradley/2025/03/21/the-human-factor-redefining-cybersecurity-in-the-age-of-ai.

System logs and suspicious activity: Are there irregular login patterns, failed login attempts, or unexpected password reset emails?

Data manipulation or leakage: Are there unexplained file changes, files moving to unexpected locations or the appearance of new files the insured didn't create?

Unfamiliar apps or messages: Are there applications the employee did not install or notice outgoing calls and messages the employee did not make?

Unexpected camera or mic activation: The camera or microphone indicator light turns on when no one is using them.[14]

Client devices are frequently the end target of the cyber breach. The router does not send instructions to the payroll service. That function belongs to the computer in the accounting department. Thus, the devices are a goldmine of information about the fraud actor's scheme. The device also contains logs that can show how and when the scheme was carried out and who was logged into the device at the time. These logs and the presence or absence of malware can substantiate—or refute—an employee's version of the events.

IX.
Web Services

So far, the discussion has been focused on devices on the insured's premises. That, however, is only part of the model. More and more, businesses are taking advantage of web services, which are modular software components that allow different applications, regardless of their operating system or programming language, to communicate and collaborate over the internet. In a business computing environment, web services act as the digital intermediaries that enable systems like inventory databases, customer relationship platforms or case-management tools to request and exchange data with one another. Businesses increasingly purchase hosted web services, such as those offered by cloud providers, instead of building and maintaining their own in-house versions.

14. Roger Grimes, 15 Signs You've Been Hacked—and How to Fight Back, CSO Online, Jan. 14, 2021, https://www.csoonline.com/article/570697/15-signs-youve-been-hacked-and-how-to-fight-back.html.

Potentially, migrating to cloud services saves on the cost and complexity of managing physical servers, in-house datacenters, software updates, scaling capacity during busy periods and round-the-clock security monitoring.[15]

The more common types of web services are Infrastructure as a Service (IaaS), Platform as a Service (PaaS) and Software as a Service (SaaS).

IaaS provides virtualized computing resources over the internet hosted by a third party. Common examples include: Amazon Web Services (AWS), which provides tools for data storage, secure file sharing, remote computing and software hosting; Microsoft Azure, which offers cloud-based tools for Identity and Access Management, secure data storage, virtual desktops, remote collaboration and application hosting; and Google's Cloud Platform, which offers services such as virtual machines, cloud storage, artificial intelligence tools and data analytics. Managing Enterprise's Directory Services, user accounts, service accounts and other computing resources in the cloud enables businesses the flexibility to operate some proprietary infrastructure on premises while synchronizing with cloud infrastructure in real time.

PaaS: This service allows organizations to build, run and manage applications without the IT infrastructure. This makes it easier and faster to develop, test and deploy applications without having to allocate internal resources, which allows developers to focus writing code and creating applications. Common PaaS Services include AWS Elastic Beanstalk or Google App Engine.

SaaS: SaaS replaces the traditional on-device software with software that is licensed on a subscription basis. It is centrally hosted in the cloud. Some examples of SaaS subscription-based applications are Salesforce (customer relationship management), QuickBooks Online (accounting), Slack (team communications), Dropbox (file sharing) and Zoom (video conferencing).[16]

As is becoming a repeated theme, even though cloud services maintain strong security protocols and employ rigorous safeguards, they are subject

---

15. Stephen J. Bigelow & Sarah Lewis, *What are web services?,* TechTarget (Mar 21, 2024), https:// www.techtarget.com/ searchapparchitecture / definition/Web-services.
16. CDW, *Top 3 Cloud Computing Service Models: IaaS vs. PaaS vs. SaaS,* CDW (Apr. 19, 2023), https://www.cdw.com/content/cdw/en/articles/cloud/top-3-cloud-computing-service-models.html.

to compromise by hackers.[17] Because these services host enormous amounts of sensitive data, they are attractive targets for cybercriminals seeking to steal data, disrupt operations, demand ransom or gain unauthorized access to confidential information. Frequently, the hackers are able to exploit misconfigured settings, stolen login credentials or unpatched software vulnerabilities rather than breaking the core infrastructure itself. For example, if a user fails to properly secure access permissions or disables multifactor authentication (MFA), that opens the door to unauthorized access, even if the platform itself remains secure.[18]

X.
Virtual Private Network Both as Victim and Attacker

A Virtual Private Network (VPN) is a secure connection method that allows users to access the internet or a private company network through an encrypted "tunnel" that protects data from being intercepted by outsiders. When a VPN is active, all internet traffic between a user's device, such as a laptop or smartphone, and the network is encrypted, meaning it is unreadable to hackers or unauthorized third parties. A VPN is especially important when employees work remotely or access confidential files over public or unsecured Wi-Fi networks. A VPN helps ensure that sensitive communications, client documents and policyholder information are kept private and protected from cyber threats. Businesses also use VPNs to secure internal resources, such as document servers or intranet sites, by restricting access to only those who connect through the VPN.[19] Today's modern networks operate VPNs on the network firewall device or appliance. By combining the security features of the firewall with the secure remote access capabilities of the VPN, businesses gain efficiency in managing these critical services.

While VPNs are designed to enhance security, they can be compromised by hackers under certain conditions, particularly if not properly configured or maintained. A hacker might target a VPN to

---

17. Microsoft Corp., *Microsoft Digital Defense Report 2024* (2024), available at https://www.microsoft.com/en-us/security/security-insider/intelligence-reports/microsoft-digital-defense-report-2024 (last visited July 13, 2025).
18. *Id.*
19. Cisco, *What Is a VPN?*, CISCO, https://www.cisco.com/c/en/us/products/security/vpn-endpoint-security-clients/what-is-vpn.html (last visited July 13, 2025).

intercept sensitive data, such as client communications, policyholder information or legal documents, as these often flow through VPNs in the legal and insurance industry. Common vulnerabilities include weak passwords, outdated VPN software and misconfigured settings, which can be exploited to gain unauthorized access. In some cases, attackers use phishing emails to trick users into revealing VPN login credentials or deploy malware to bypass security protections. Hackers are especially motivated to compromise business VPNs because doing so could grant them access to the broader company network, including confidential records and financial systems.

Just as legitimate users rely on VPNs to protect their privacy and encrypt their communications, cybercriminals use the same technology to hide their identities, locations and online activities while launching attacks. By routing their traffic through VPNs—often through multiple countries—hackers make it extremely difficult for investigators to trace the source of an attack. This anonymity is particularly useful when conducting phishing campaigns, installing malware or probing a network for vulnerabilities. In some cases, attackers even use stolen VPN credentials from a legitimate business user to gain undetected access to internal systems. According to the cybersecurity firm Palo Alto Networks, attackers increasingly use "legitimate services like VPNs to mask their origin and avoid detection by traditional network monitoring tools."[20]

XI. Conclusion

This chapter is by no means an exhaustive discourse covering the business computing environment. It is intended to arm the reader with the knowledge to better understand how to identify compromised components, understand breach mechanisms and assess the impact on data and services. As businesses increasingly digitize, the ability to navigate technical aspects becomes vital for accurate risk assessment and informed decision-making. As noted at the beginning of this article, coverage under crime policies, financial institution bonds and other types of fidelity policies often depends on identifying who executed the scheme and how it was carried out. By gaining a deeper understanding of the business

20. *See, e.g.*, Bulletproof, *How Hackers Hide: VPNs, Proxies, and the Art of Anonymity*, Bulletproof Blog (Mar. 15, 2022), https://www.bulletproof.co.uk/blog/how-hackers-hide.

computing environment, the insurance professional is better equipped to ask more pertinent questions that yield the most useful information, which can be applied to the coverage analysis.

CHAPTER 5

COMPUTER SECURITY TECHNOLOGY—MODERN TRENDS AND TOOLS TO DEFEND AGAINST CYBER CRIME

Christopher Ballod

I. Introduction

Cybercrime is on the rise. For example, incidents known as "ransomware attacks" continue to grow exponentially, with a sharp uptick occurring in summer 2025. "Ransomware" is a label for a type of extortionate attack where the threat actor gains access to a computer network and then encrypts data, making it unusable until a ransom is paid for a decryption key. The threat actor almost always copies key data as well, threatening to publish it on their publication site if the ransom is not paid. This sharp increase is significant because summer months are typically slower for this type of cybercrime, leading many experts to be concerned that the typically busiest time—the months from September through December—could reach crisis levels.

A further increase in cybercrime can only mean that the unprepared will have a very high likelihood of experiencing a catastrophic incident. All business sectors are more digitized than ever. Law firms, for example, have digitized case files, client communications, court submissions, and even sensitive personal data existing on interconnected systems. This connectivity brings unprecedented convenience, but it also increases the attack surface for cybercriminals. By understanding the threats, the possible solutions, and the potential fallout from a catastrophic incident, some of this harm may be avoided or minimized.

II.
The Threats

The most common—and most damaging—threats include:

Business Email Compromise (BEC)

BEC attacks target email accounts to impersonate clients, vendors, or executives, often to redirect payments or obtain sensitive data. A single successful BEC attack can result in devastating financial losses and reputational harm.

Extortionate Attacks

These include ransomware, where access to systems is locked until a ransom is paid, and data extortion, where individuals threaten to publicly release stolen client data unless demands are met. They are typically conducted in a manner to avoid detection until the threat actor is ready to demand a ransom.

Insider Threats, Hacktivists, and Nation States

A disgruntled employee, politically motivated group, or foreign intelligence service may pursue access for purposes far beyond simple theft. Each poses unique investigative and legal challenges.

That is not to say that these are the only threats. There are threats to the well-being of individuals by preying on vulnerabilities through social media, threats to the integrity of operations by defacing websites, and even threats to infrastructure caused by commandeering resources for other nefarious activities.

III.
The Defenses—The "Human Firewall"

Technology alone cannot secure a business in 2025. Even the most advanced security infrastructure can be defeated if an employee inadvertently grants access to a threat actor. Businesses must be aware of threats and train their employees to be aware as well, by employing a number of approaches:

Implement Employee Training

- Conduct phishing awareness training twice a year, with quarterly simulated phishing tests.

- Treat test failures as learning opportunities, unless repeated failures indicate negligence.
- Teach staff how to identify common manipulation tactics: e.g. urgency, authority impersonation, and requests for secrecy.

Recognize Deep Fakes

- Audio deep fakes are more common than video; many are deployed over phone calls.
- In video meetings, verify identities—especially if requests involve sensitive actions—by asking participants to turn cameras on.
- If an impersonated individual has an extensive public video or audio footprint, they are at higher risk of deep fake targeting.

Implement Verification Procedures

- Develop out-of-band verification procedures that require contacting a pre-determined individual at a pre-determined number to verify requested actions.

Adopt "Know Your Customer"–style protocols:

- End any call or meeting where sensitive requests are made and reinitiate contact through a pre-established, verified channel.
- Never rely solely on the method of communication provided by the requester.

Limit Access ("Least Privilege Principle")

- Individual staff members should have access only to data required for his or her daily tasks.
- Review access privileges regularly.

Assess Your IT Team

- Ensure you have dedicated security expertise in-house or through a managed provider.
- Consider segregation of duties; in 2025, it is rare for one person to effectively handle both IT operations and security responsibilities.

Review Data Inventory and Retention

- Know what data you store, where it resides, and how long it must be retained.
- Delete what you do not need—data you do not have cannot be stolen.

Use Backups

- Maintain a "golden copy" of essential business or legally mandated data offline.
- Test backup restoration regularly.

Review Security Controls

- Maintain accurate asset inventories. You can only defend what you know about and control.
- Remove local administrator rights from user devices.
- Patch internet-facing systems promptly, and monitor systems for zero-day vulnerabilities.

Conduct Incident Response Planning

- Store your incident response plan offline.
- Define what constitutes an incident, who leads the response, and who manages internal and external communications.
- Identify vendors for forensic investigation, remediation, negotiations, and notification before a crisis occurs.

Manage Accounts

- Enforce password complexity: minimum 13 characters (18 preferred) with numbers, upper- and lower-case letters, and symbols.
- Use password managers after vetting for security and ease of use.
- Require Multi-Factor Authentication (MFA) for all accounts, understanding that it is not foolproof but remains a critical defense.
- Secure service accounts which often cannot use MFA and are easily overlooked.

Employ Data Segmentation

- Store sensitive data separately and behind multiple authentication layers.
- Use different credentials for email and sensitive systems.

Use Managed Detection and Response (MDR)

- MDR tools, backed by a 24/7 Security Operations Center, are some of the few tools capable of detecting intrusions in progress, but they are not infallible and can be costly.

While implementing these protections may require significant investments of time and expense, threat actors are investing substantial resources in efforts to evade system security.

IV.
How Threat Actors Are Succeeding

No matter how robust your security posture, the threat actors only need to find one way in, one time, whereas the defenders must be successful every time. Three techniques by threat actors are prevalent in 2025:

Social Engineering.

Advanced phishing techniques, deep fakes, and supply chain compromises are on the rise. Most people are familiar with "phishing"—those deceptive emails or texts pretending to be from a trusted source, designed to trick you into revealing your login information. But threat actors in recent years have upgraded this scam with something more sophisticated: the man-in-the-middle attack. The attacker sends a link (via email, text, or even a calendar invite) that looks like it leads to a normal login screen for email, case management software, or cloud storage. In actuality the link directs to the attacker's special web page—a fake "front desk" they control. This fake page does not just steal credentials, it acts as a go-between with the legitimate website so the user is not alerted. When the user enters credentials, the attacker's system immediately sends it to the real website. If the real website then asks for an MFA code (like a number texted to the user or generated by an app), the fake page asks for it too—in real time—and passes it right along. Because this all happens instantly, the attacker uses both the password and the one-time MFA code before it expires, logging into the real account as if they were the user.

Vulnerability Exploitation

Threat actors actively scan for unpatched systems and zero-day exploits. Every piece of software and hardware that touches the internet could have a flaw in the code that allows a threat actor to do something simple and gain access to it or through it. The threat actors work at finding new exploits constantly. Manufacturers must be alerted to an exploit, generate a patch that fixes it, and then alert users. In the meantime, the threat actors are in and stealing credentials or doing other things to make sure they can maintain access or return later. Threat actors find vulnerable systems easily by searching internet-connected devices with web crawling bots or "internet of things" search engines.

"Watering Hole"/"Drive-By Attacks"

Compromising trusted third-party websites to deliver malware via scripting. The user may be given an innocuous pop up to interact with that enables the scripting, but some variations of this attack do not even require user interaction. Recently, we have observed threat actors targeting golf league websites for this technique. When an executive at a victim enterprise downloads and executes the malware, the threat actor is alerted and uses that executive's computer as a jumping off point for a ransomware attack.

V.
The Consequences: What a Catastrophic Incident Could Look Like

To truly get a sense of the risk/reward analysis, a business must understand the potential consequences of these incidents.

Immediate Financial Loss

The goal of BEC threat actors is to monetize the effort by redirecting a payment of some kind. If they succeed either the business they compromised will pay money to the wrong party (the threat actor) and still owe the money to the legitimate recipient, or the business will not receive money it is owed. Often a business that transfers a payment to a threat actor, instead of the legitimate recipient, will not have the means to simply reissue the payment. In the case of employees whose payroll has been redirected, that error could be catastrophic for mortgage payments, tuition, and other essential budget items.

Business Interruption and Reputational Harm

Often hard to quantify, the disruption to the business can last only weeks in the best-case scenarios, and several months in some of the worst-case scenarios. Some businesses have not recovered at all from the loss of critical data or damage to client relationships. There is no easy metric for this since a lot of the harm is unique to the situation the business was in prior to the incident, but it is safe to say that this is typically a significant number.

Costs Associated with the Incident Response

Businesses that try to respond to an incident without help often find themselves seeking help after the incident has been exacerbated, or finding out that auditors, regulators, or sophisticated customers and vendors react poorly to the absence of an independent investigation. A full incident response team often includes:

- Privacy counsel (often called a "breach coach"). Privacy counsel provide legal advice, protect the incident response activities with the attorney-client privilege, prepare internal and external communications, direct the investigation, and coordinate the other vendors' activities.
- Digital forensics/incident response (DFIR). DFIR secures the computer environment and investigates to determine what the threat actor accomplished and the universe of potential data-at-risk.
- Recovery/Remediation. Vendors restore or rebuild impacted systems, assist with data collection for the investigation, and assist the client with security hardening.
- Negotiator. If the matter involves an extortionate threat actor, the negotiator will conduct negotiations akin to hostage negotiations where they will, at a minimum, attempt to gain information about what the threat actor stole, and their ability to decrypt the encrypted data. These negotiations also serve to delay further threat actor actions.
- Notification. If protected data sets are compromised in the incident, notifications could be required by law. For any size notification population, a vendor specializing in printing and mailing the notifications, and managing a call center to support the likely calls from recipients, may be required.

Litigation and/or Regulatory Fines and Penalties

There is no national privacy law in the United States. It is a patchwork of state laws and regulatory frameworks. If a notification is required, some states also require regulatory notification. Some regulators publish information about reporting entities on their websites. That information is often used by the class action bar to pursue information about potential lawsuits. We are seeing a very large spike in the volume of litigation filed as a result of cybersecurity incidents. With the ever-increasing number of regulators creating their own rules for reporting and enforcement, this is a complicated and costly risk.

VI.
Checklist: Cybersecurity Best Practices

- Conduct biannual phishing training and quarterly simulations.
- Limit access to "least privilege" levels.
- Maintain a complete inventory of data and IT assets.

- Implement and test offline backups.
- Remove local administrator rights from user devices.
- Monitor and patch internet-facing systems quickly.
- Enforce strong passwords and use MFA everywhere possible.
- Secure and monitor service accounts.
- Segment sensitive data with layered authentication.
- Consider MDR with 24/7 SOC coverage.
- Develop an incident response plan and keep it available offline.

VII.
Conclusion

In many industries, cybersecurity is not merely an IT concern—it is a core responsibility. The trust of customers and key vendors depends on the integrity and confidentiality of their information. In an era of sophisticated and persistent threats, protecting that trust requires continuous vigilance, layered defenses, and above all, a culture where every employee is part of the security team.

CHAPTER 6

FUNDS TRANSFER FRAUD— A PRACTICAL APPROACH

Jennifer Bollinger
J. Caralisa Connell
Brian Rice

I. Introduction

In this technological era, computers have become an integral part of how society functions at the business level. Businesses seldom can operate without relying on computers in most, if not all, aspects of the business including consumer transactions, banking, communications, and payroll. Unsurprisingly, as computer usage has increased, so has the number of fraudsters using computers to commit crimes. With the ever-increasing amount of computer crime, the insurance industry began introducing certain computer or technology related insuring agreements. One of these insuring agreements is often referred to as the funds transfer fraud insuring agreement.

Funds transfer fraud insuring agreements were introduced, and sometimes still are written, as a corollary to the computer fraud coverage. However, the computer fraud coverage is intended to cover hacking incidents coupled with a fraudulent transfer, where the funds transfer fraud coverage is aimed at protecting a separate and distinct risk: situations where a fraudster induces a financial institution to allow funds to be withdrawn from the insured's account by posing as the insured and submitting fraudulent instructions.

While funds transfer fraud only provides coverage for a limited type of risk, fraudsters have continued to evolve, becoming more and more sophisticated in their schemes. In today's world fraudsters are using numerous types of schemes to pose as the insured and submit fraudulent instructions including, but not limited to, hacking to obtain information, phishing emails, impersonation, and business email compromise. Though not all of these schemes implicate coverage under funds transfer fraud insuring agreements, they all contribute to the technological landscape of computer crime and claims submitted by insureds under funds transfer fraud insuring agreements. This chapter will include a practical discussion of funds transfer fraud language and coverage, underwriting issues related to funds transfer fraud risks, and the technology and schemes related to funds transfer fraud.

II.
Funds Transfer Fraud Coverage—Policy Forms

Funds transfer fraud coverage, while consistently included in commercial crime policies, can vary in form and language across policies. For example, the Insurance Services Organization's 2015 Commercial Crime Policy[1] provides coverage for funds transfer fraud in a single insuring agreement with computer fraud coverage titled "Computer and Funds Transfer Fraud."[2] The funds transfer fraud portion of the "Computer and Funds Transfer Fraud" insuring agreement states:

> a. We will pay for:
> (2) Loss resulting directly from a "fraudulent instruction" directing a "financial institution" to debit your "transfer account" and to transfer, pay or deliver "money" or "securities" from that account.

The 2015 ISO CCP further defines "Fraudulent Instruction" to mean:

> a. With regard to Insuring Agreement A.6.a.(2):
> (1) A computer, telefacsimile, telephone or other electronic instruction directing a "financial institution" to debit your "transfer account" and to transfer, pay or deliver "money" or "securities" from that "transfer account," which instruction purports to have been issued by you, but which in fact was

1. Hereinafter referred to as "2015 ISO CCP."
2. Commercial Crime Policy, CR 00 22 11 15 (ISO Props., Inc. 2015)

fraudulently issued by someone else without your knowledge or consent; or

(2) A written instruction (other than those coverage under Insuring Agreement A.2.) issued to a "financial institution" to debit your "transfer account" and to transfer, pay or deliver "money" or "securities" from the "transfer account," through an electronic funds transfer system at specified times or under specified conditions, which instruction purports to have been issued by you, but which in fact was issued, forged or altered by someone else without your knowledge or consent.

Other policy forms provide for funds transfer fraud as a standalone insuring agreement. For instance, the Surety and Fidelity Association of America's 2019 Crime Protection Policy's Funds Transfer Fraud insuring agreement provides:

> We will pay for loss of funds resulting directly from a fraudulent instruction directing a financial institution to transfer, pay or deliver funds from your transfer account.[3]

The 2019 SFAA CCP further defines fraudulent instruction to mean:

a. A payment order transmitted to a financial institution which purports to have been transmitted by you, but which was in fact fraudulently transmitted by someone else without your knowledge or consent; or
b. A written instruction (other than those described by Insuring Agreement 2.) which purports to have been issued by you and which was sent or transmitted to a financial institution through an electronic funds transfer system and which was issued, forged or altered without your knowledge or consent.

Manuscript forms may also provide funds transfer coverage in varying formats. One typical example of manuscript coverage provided by a funds transfer fraud insuring agreement is as follows:

---

3. Crime Protection Policy, SP 00 01 03 19 (SFAA 2019) (available from SFAA) (hereinafter referred to as "2019 SFAA CPP").

> The Insurer shall pay for loss of **Money** or **Securities** sustained by an **Insured** resulting directly from **Funds Transfer Fraud** committed by a **Third Party**.

Funds Transfer Fraud is then defined to mean:

> [F]raudulent electronic, telegraphic, cable, teletype, facsimile, telephone or written instructions (other than **Forgery**) purportedly issued by an **Insured** to a **Financial Institution** by a **Third Party** which directs such **Financial Institution**, which in reliance upon said instruction transfers, pays, or delivers **Money** or **Securities** from any account maintained by such **Insured** at such financial institution to a person, place, or account beyond the **Insured's** control, without such **Insured's** knowledge or consent.

While these forms take slightly varying approaches to their respective funds transfer fraud coverage, the coverage provided varies very little, if at all. Under each insuring agreement, establishing funds transfer fraud coverage still requires that a third party purport to be the insured and issue a fraudulent instruction directly to a financial institution without the insured's knowledge or consent.

III.
Technology Related to Funds Transfer Fraud

Funds transfer fraud has evolved far beyond the days of clumsy and obvious phishing emails and poorly translated scams with glaring spelling and grammatical issues. The Nigerian princes of yesterday have evolved dramatically. Funds transfer fraud has now become a $1.6 trillion enterprise, with domestic losses pegged at $12.5 billion in 2024, a 25% jump from 2023. Today's schemes are powered by a sophisticated criminal ecosystem that exploits both technological vulnerabilities and human trust. Bad actors are not just the kid down the street living in mom's house; they are also state-sponsored with direct links to China, North Korea, Russia, and other countries. These bad actors are not only evolving rapidly with the help of artificial intelligence (AI) but also have access to helpdesk-for-a-fee services, which enable them to coordinate group attacks and perform level two and three triage, thereby facilitating more sophisticated and damaging attacks.

Bad actors leverage stolen credentials, access-for-sale brokerage houses, cloud identity systems, collaboration platforms, and real-time payment rails to turn small gaps into multimillion-dollar issues on an hourly basis. To understand the modern and evolving threat, we must examine how these schemes operate, the exploited technologies, and defenses available to underwriters, claims professionals, and insureds.

A. How the Schemes Work

Most incidents begin with an identity compromise, which will then be used to target email systems primarily. The easiest entry point is to exploit the human trust factor, not try to break firewalls or proximity security systems. The human trust factor is the lowest-hanging fruit that is easily picked. Bad actors easily deploy adversary-in-the-middle (AiTM) phishing kits, such as EvilProxy or Evilginx (readily available for free downloads on the dark web), which not only harvest credentials but also capture live multi-factor authentication tokens. This allows criminals to hijack sessions and persist in the victim's account without detection. Once inside, the attacker sets inbox rules and forwarding mechanisms to intercept or conceal legitimate correspondence. In more advanced cases, victims are tricked into granting OAuth consent to malicious applications, which provide long-term access to email and files – even after a password reset.

With this foothold, attackers monitor business communications until the right opportunity arises. The average amount of time before a bad actor makes their move is 277 days. That's correct—277 days is the average time between an entry and an event. Once they choose to act, the bad actors then insert fraudulent payment instructions into a legitimate transaction, redirecting funds to accounts under their control. Or, more simply, they will adjust the ACH and account numbers on an existing PDF and send this information to the unsuspecting financial institution.

Increasingly, fraudsters and bad actors use AI-generated deepfakes to reinforce credibility. It is incredibly easy to utilize AI to mimic the tone of an email, the voice of a superior, or truthfully the voice of anyone. You do not have to look far to find these types of AI-generated deepfakes and even government employees, like Marco Rubio,[4] find themselves in the news for these incidents.

---

4. Sharon Goldman, *How a deepfake of Marco Rubio exposed the alarming ease of AI voice scams*, FORTUNE, https://fortune.com/2025/07/10/deepfake-marco-rubio-ai-voice-scams/ (published July 10, 2025).

In one widely reported case, criminals in Hong Kong used a deepfake video call to impersonate a Chief Financial Officer, persuading employees to authorize transfers exceeding $25 million.[5] This convergence of social engineering and synthetically generated media marks a dangerous escalation in the threat landscape.

B. Technologies Being Exploited

The effectiveness of these schemes is rooted in structural weaknesses at both the identity and payments layers. Most organizations continue to rely on outdated email authentication or allow insecure legacy protocols, creating fertile ground for spoofing and unauthorized access. Where Domain-based Message Authentication, Reporting, and Conformance (DMARC), Sender Policy Framework (SPF), and DomainKeys Identified Mail (DKIM) are not fully enforced, attackers can directly impersonate trusted domains with relative ease.

Payment systems themselves are often unforgiving. FedNow and other real-time payment (RTP) networks settle transactions within seconds, with no practical mechanism for reversal once funds are released. Wire transfers governed by UCC Article 4A are similarly final once the beneficiary's bank accepts the payment, with cancellation allowed only in narrow, exceptional circumstances. Even ACH payments, often perceived as more flexible, allow only limited return windows for businesses, typically within two banking days for errors, while consumers have longer to dispute rights. The Electronic Funds Transfer Act (EFTA) aims to ensure individuals are well-informed about their rights and protections, which should also be regularly reviewed. Bad actors understand these timelines intimately and exploit them to ensure stolen funds move beyond recovery before victims even realize what has happened.

C. Practical Defenses

With all of these new and improved risks, how can insureds (and insurers) protect themselves? It is critical for insurers to understand the computer and cyber-based controls an insured has in place to properly

---

5. Cheng Leng and Chan Ho-Him, *Arup lost $25mn in Hong Kong deepfake video conference scam*, FINANCIAL TIMES, https:/www.ft.com/content/b977e8d4-664c-4ae4-8a8e-eb93bdf785ea (published May 16, 2024).

assess the risk of loss from funds transfer fraud.[6] For insureds, a layered defense strategy is essential. From a technical standpoint, organizations should:

- Have a strong cyber hygiene program across the board and employ a managed security services provider (MSSP).
- Enforce DMARC with a reject policy, disable legacy authentication protocols, and prohibit automatic external forwarding.
- Set up inbound email security systems (Avanan, Microsoft Defender, Proofpoint, Mimecast, Barracuda, or similar).
- Utilize Domain Name System (DNS) filtering to block malicious URLs inadvertently typed in, clicked on, or pushed via phishing emails, typosquatting, or hijacked URLs or websites.
- Deploy strong Endpoint Detection and Response (EDR) and Extended Detection and Response (XDR) to mitigate risks from deployed ransomware, keyloggers, or others.
- Require phishing-resistant multi-factor authentication (such as hardware tokens for FIDO2/WebAuthn credentials) for financial staff and administrators.
- Restrict or monitor OAuth application consent, forcing administrator approval for third-party integrations and conducting regular reviews.
- Enable continuous mailbox auditing and anomaly detection to identify suspicious sign-ins or rule changes.
- Place EXTERNAL email banners on emails to bring attention to any emails that look like they are coming from an internal employee, but are not, because of domain authentication or other techniques.
- DarkWebMonitoring for company domains is critical, as alerts will be sent as soon as stolen credentials show up on the dark web from any breach.
- Mandatory Access Control Lists and deployed Network Access Policies (and strict logging), utilizing the law of least privilege for any systems containing Personal Identifying Information (PII) or Payment Card Industry Information (PCI).
- Quarterly employee cyber security awareness training is a must!

---

6. Important underwriting considerations are discussed in more detail in Section IV.

Equally important are payment process controls. Out-of-band verification—confirming instructions through a trusted phone number already on record, not one provided in an email—is indispensable. Although, sadly, it is also very easy to spoof phone numbers. Dual authorization for new or modified beneficiaries adds another critical layer. Some organizations introduce "hold periods" for first-time payments, creating a short delay that can buy precious hours to detect fraud before money becomes unrecoverable.

D. The Reality Check

The scale of the problem is staggering. According to the FBI's Internet Crime Complaint Center, business email compromise (BEC) schemes accounted for adjusted losses of $12.5 billion for funds transfer fraud alone and well over $16.6 billion in other BEC compromises in 2023,[7] making them the single most costly category of cyber-enabled crime.[8] These are not fringe incidents; they represent a central risk in modern financial fraud. With the convergence of advanced identity exploitation, artificial intelligence, and real-time settlement systems, the challenge is only accelerating.

In the ongoing and escalating fight against funds transfer fraud, organizations must learn to trust identities less and payments least. Third party audits for cyber defense protocols are becoming a critical component to mitigate losses and litigation expenses, and are becoming a clear winner in the overwhelming fight. Technology may drive the schemes, but disciplined controls and vigilant oversight remain the best defense.

---

7. *New FTC Data Show a Big Jump in Reported Losses to Fraud to $12.5 Billion in 2024*, Federal Trade Commission, https://www.ftc.gov/news-events/news/press-releases/2025/03/new-ftc-data-show-big-jump-reported-losses-fraud-125-billion-2024 (last visited Aug. 18, 2025).
8. Federal Bureau of Investigation Internet Crime Report 2024, available at https://www.ic3.gov/AnnualReport/Reports/2024_IC3Report.pdf (last visited Aug. 18, 2025).

IV.
Underwriting Issues Related to Funds Transfer Fraud

Now that we have discussed a basic understanding of the technological aspects of funds transfer fraud, the next question is how to analyze the risk through underwriting. As with all insuring agreements, there are certain risks that insurers are hesitant or unwilling to cover related to funds transfer fraud coverage. It is imperative that insurers understand the insured's risk factors related to funds transfer fraud coverage, and other electronic coverages, prior to issuing policies including these electronic coverages. There are a number of important topics that should be reviewed in order to understand the risks associated with an insured potentially suffering funds transfer fraud.

The potential risk an insured has for sustaining a loss resulting directly from funds transfer fraud can be evaluated through a number of questions that are commonly included on crime insurance applications, as well as some follow-up questions that may provide additional insight into the insured's risk landscape especially with respect to cyber health and internal controls. Some examples of important and pertinent questions include:

- What is the insured's class of business?
- Does the insured hold funds on behalf of its clients? If so, does the insured transfer funds on behalf of clients?
- How many daily transactions does the insured process?
- What is the average and maximum dollar amount transferred by the insured?
- What controls does the insured have in place for transfers? Does the insured require dual authorization? Does the insured have the bank call someone other than the person who made the transfer request to confirm the transfer?
- What security controls does the insured have in place? Does the insured require multi-factor authentication? Has the insured installed all current upgrades and patches?
- What computer or cyber-based controls does the insured have in place?
- Has the insured suffered similar incidents or losses previously? If so, how did those incidents or losses occur, did the loss occur because established controls were circumvented or because

appropriate controls were not in place, and what changes were implemented to prevent future incidents or losses?

These questions are regularly included on insurance applications in some form. But, from an underwriting perspective, evaluating an insured's potential exposure involves more than just base-level considerations—especially in the case of large organizations. Additional questions should probe the insured's identity and payment control environment. For instance, does the insured enforce DMARC at a reject level? Have they disabled legacy login protocols and external forwarding? Do they use phishing-resistant MFA? Is there a documented process for verifying vendor account changes, and does it include both technological and human safeguards? Do they employ and regularly test their cyber hygiene protocols as outlined above? Finally, do they operate on rails like FedNow or RTP, where recall is functionally impossible, or are they still primarily relying on ACH and wire transfers? In-depth audits, while invasive and subject to significant pushback, are highly encouraged and recommended—especially when an insured is seeking significant limits of insurance. Why underwrite an insured who will most certainly have an incident and claim due to lack of security?

Additionally, it is helpful to understand the impetus for the insured's need for funds transfer fraud coverage. On occasion, insured's clients, or prospective clients, will have contractual requirements for certain risks including, but not limited to, computer crime. Some of those contractual requirements *may* implicate funds transfer fraud coverage. However, the contractual requirements often lend themselves more readily to other electronic coverages such as computer fraud or social engineering. As discussed in more detail in this chapter, the funds transfer fraud provides relatively limited coverage for a very specific situation. To that end, it is important to ensure that brokers, the insured, and the insured's prospective clients understand the difference between funds transfer fraud coverage and social engineering coverage. Understanding these items can help to alleviate common issues that arise later in the life of a policy.

V.
Funds Transfer Fraud Coverage and Claims

While funds transfer fraud claims appear to be on the rise along with other electronic- and cybercrime-based claims, there remains very little case law analyzing these provisions. Often times, funds transfer fraud claims appear in the form of a "tag-along" to a computer fraud or social engineering claim. In other words, an insured submits a claim for computer fraud or social engineering and also seeks coverage under funds transfer fraud. When analyzing claims for coverage, it is important to focus on the different requirements under funds transfer fraud than other insuring agreements. The most typical issues that arise in conjunction with these claims are (1) the definition of fraudulent instruction including whether the instruction was sent from the fraudster to the bank directly; (2) whether the insured suffered a direct loss from funds transfer fraud; or (3) whether a relevant exclusion applies.

A. Fraudulent Instruction

The vast majority of funds transfer fraud claims, and the case law interpreting such claims, hinge on whether a fraudulent instruction occurred. There have been two relatively recent federal circuit court cases that have discussed this issue. In *Valero Title Inc. v. RLI Insurance Co.*,[9] the insured purchased a funds transfer fraud endorsement that provided "we will pay for loss of funds resulting directly from a fraudulent instruction direction [sic] financial institution to transfer, pay or deliver funds from your transfer account." The policy defined "fraudulent instruction" as "[a] written instruction . . . issued by you, which was forged or altered by someone other than you without your knowledge or consent, or which purports to have been issued by you, but was in fact fraudulently issued without your knowledge or consent."

The insured had suffered a loss after its employee discussed a loan payoff transaction over email with a lender's employee. A fraudster posed as the lender's employee and sent the insured fraudulent wiring instructions with a fraudulent routing number. The insured's employee then instructed the insured's bank to wire money pursuant to the fraudulent wiring instructions. The insured submitted a claim under the funds transfer fraud endorsement.

The United States Court of Appeals for the Fifth Circuit held that coverage existed for the insured's loss. In making its determination, the court looked to the definition of fraudulent instruction and noted that it had two clauses "Clause A" and "Clause B." "Clause A" states, "a written instruction . . . issued by you, which was forged or altered by someone

9. No. 22-20155, 2023 WL 1434270 (5th Cir. Feb. 1, 2023).

other than you without your knowledge or consent." While "Clause B" states, "a written instruction . . . which purports to have been issued by you, but was in fact fraudulently issued without your knowledge or consent." The court ultimately determined that "the only interpretation of Clause A that does not render Clause B meaningless is one in which a written instruction is forged or altered by someone other than the insured without the insured's knowledge or consent prior to being issued by the insured."

Thus, the court in *Valero Title* found coverage for what was seemingly a social engineering based scheme under the funds transfer fraud insuring agreement. However, it is important to note that while it is expected that this case will be cited in favor of coverage for social engineering schemes under funds transfer fraud coverages, the case should be easily distinguishable from the standard form funds transfer fraud coverages discussed above. The policy in *Valero Title* was a significantly older form. The 2015 ISO CCP and the 2019 SFAA CPP, as well as most manuscript policies on the market today, have eliminated any language akin to "Clause A" in the *Valero Title* policy, and instead only contain language requiring the instruction purport to have been issued by you.

Another relevant funds transfer fraud case is *Ernst & Haas Management, Co., Inc. v. Hiscox*,[10] which was decided by the United States Court of Appeals for the Ninth Circuit. In *Ernst*, the insured's accounts payable clerk received an email purporting to be from her superior directing her to make a payment. Unbeknownst to the accounts payable clerk, the email was not from her superior, but was instead from a fraudulent actor. The accounts payable clerk processed the payment by wire transfer based on the payment instructions received from the fraudulent actor. The clerk received two more email instructions from the fraudulent actor and made one more wire transfer before emailing her superior directly to confirm the authenticity of the invoice and payment request. After learning that her superior did not request the payments, the insured attempted to recover the payments, but they had already been completed.

The insured sought coverage under a commercial crime policy under both prongs of the policy's Computer and Funds Transfer Fraud insuring agreement. The court ultimately determined that the insured's claim was "likely covered" under the funds transfer fraud provision. The court

10. 23 F.4th 1195 (9th Cir. 2022).

reasoned that the definition of fraudulent instruction included a definition stating "an electronic . . . instruction initially received by You which purports to have been transmitted by an Employee but which was in fact fraudulently transmitted by someone else without Your or the Employee's knowledge or consent." Thus, similarly to *Valero Title*, the court's decision hinged on the fact that the policy anticipated an instruction sent to the insured before the bank and any other interpretation would cause that language to be superfluous. Again, it is important to note that the determining language in *Ernst* is not present in the current standard forms and thus, policies may be easily distinguishable from *Ernst*.[11]

B. Direct Loss

Another consistent issue that arises in funds transfer fraud claims is whether the insured suffered a loss resulting directly from funds transfer fraud. The causation required in commercial crime policies has been an oft litigated and examined topic.[12] Thus, this chapter will only discuss direct loss and causation in brief as it has been applied specifically to funds transfer fraud coverage. There is a dearth case law discussing causation or direct loss with respect to funds transfer fraud.[13] The standard form

---

11. Other reference books have compiled thorough surveys of cases discussing the meaning of fraudulent instruction under funds transfer fraud coverage. *See* J. Caralisa Connell, Justin D. Wear & Michael Branley, *Funds Transfer Fraud Insuring Agreement, in* THE FINANCIAL INSTITUTION BOND AND COMMERCIAL CRIME POLICY: PRINCIPLES AND ANNOTATIONS, 529-535 (Michael Keeley, et al., eds., 2024).

12. *See, i.e.*, Gary J. Valeriano, *Direct Loss and Causation, in* COMMERCIAL CRIME INSURANCE COVERAGE, 351 (Randall I. Marmor & Susan Koehler Sullivan, eds., 2015); Scott L. Schmookler & Meagan P. VanderWeele, *Causation, Direct Loss, and Third-Party Loss, in* THE FINANCIAL INSTITUTION BOND AND COMMERCIAL CRIME POLICY: PRINCIPLES AND ANNOTATIONS, 815 (Michael Keeley, et al., eds., 2024); Scott Schmookler, Courtney Nichol and Sarah Riedl Clark, *Causation and Third-Party Loss, in* HANDLING FIDELITY BOND CLAIMS (Michael Keeley, et al., eds. 2019).

13. As discussed earlier in this chapter, funds transfer fraud coverage claims have not been litigated in significant numbers and often are brought as a tag-along to computer fraud coverage claims. Thus, while there are many cases discussing the causation and direct loss requirements of computer coverage, there are few cases that specifically discuss causation and direct

policies require that the insured suffered a loss resulting directly from funds transfer fraud. Because the insured's loss must be direct, it is important to understand how the insured's loss occurred from a technological standpoint to better determine whether such loss was in fact direct.

C. Common Exclusions Applicable to Funds Transfer Fraud Claims

There are a few exclusions that may be implicated by funds transfer fraud claims to keep in mind when evaluating whether coverage exists for a claim. These exclusions include the authorized representative exclusion, the voluntary parting and/or the exchange or purchases exclusion, the confidential information exclusion, and funneling exclusions.

Under the authorized representative exclusion, even if an insured establishes funds transfer fraud, the loss may be excluded if it was caused by an employee's theft or dishonest conduct. An example of the authorized representative exclusion is as follows:

> Loss resulting from "theft" or any other dishonest act committed by any of your "employees", "managers", directors, trustees or authorized representatives:
>
> (1) Whether acting alone or in collusion with other persons; or
>
> (2) While performing services for you or otherwise;
>
> except when covered under Insuring Agreement A.1.[14]

Additionally, commercial crime policies frequently include voluntary parting or exchange or purchases exclusions. An example of these types of exclusions are as follows:

> **Exchange or Purchase**
>
> Loss resulting from the giving or surrendering of property in any exchange or purchase.

---

loss as it pertains to the funds transfer fraud coverage. *See* Principle Sol. Grp., LLC v. Ironshore Indem., Inc., 944 F.3d 886, 892 (11th Cir. 2019).

14. Commercial Crime Policy, CR 00 22 11 15 (ISO Props., Inc. 2015).

> **Voluntary Parting of Title to or Possession of Property**
> Loss resulting from the **Insured**, or anyone acting on the **Insured's** express or implied authority, being induced by any dishonest act to part voluntarily with title to or possession of any property.[15]

In certain funds transfer fraud coverage scenarios, these exclusions may apply to exclude coverage. However, it is important to note that some policies do not contain both of these exclusions, or these exclusions are only applicable to certain insuring agreements, which may or may not include funds transfer fraud.

Another potentially applicable exclusion is the confidential information exclusion. For example, Insurance Services Organizations 2012 Commercial Crime Policy[16] excludes coverage for:

> Loss resulting from:
> (1) The disclosure of your or another person's or organization's confidential or personal information including, but not limited to, patents, trade secrets, processing methods, customer lists, financial information, credit card information, health information or any other type of nonpublic information; or
> (2) The use of another person's or organization's confidential or personal information including, but not limited to, patents, trade secrets, processing methods, customer lists, financial information, credit card information, health information or any other type of nonpublic information.

As discussed above, fraudsters may sit in an insured's computer systems for some time collecting nonpublic or sensitive information. The collected nonpublic or confidential information is then used to perpetrate the relevant frauds. The confidential information exclusion could exclude coverage in those instances where an insured's loss results from the use or disclosure of that nonpublic or confidential information.

However, in recent years, many insurers have introduced new language that may take many fact patterns related to funds transfer fraud

---

15. Crime Protection Policy, SP 00 01 03 19 (SFAA 2019) (available from SFAA).
16. Commercial Crime Policy, CR 00 22 08 13 (ISO Props, Inc. 2012).

out of the scope of the confidential information exclusion.[17] Many policies, such as the 2015 ISO CCP, contain revised language that excludes coverage for:

> Loss resulting from:
> (1) The disclosure or use of another person's or organization's confidential or personal information; or
> (2) The disclosure of your confidential or personal information. However, this **Paragraph 1.d.(2)** does not apply to loss otherwise covered under this Policy that results directly from the use of your confidential or personal information.[18]

Some insurers have further modified the language. An example of these further modifications is as follows:

> Confidential Information
> (i) Loss involving the disclosure or use of an **Insured's** or another entity or person's **Confidential Information** while in the care, custody, or control of an **Insured**; or
> (ii) fees, costs, fines, penalties, or any other expenses incurred by an **Insured** which result, directly or indirectly, from the access to or disclosure of **Confidential Information**,
>
> provided, this Exclusion shall not apply to loss that is otherwise covered under this Policy through the use of **Confidential Information** to facilitate such loss;

Accordingly, while some policies exclude loss from fact patterns that may implicate funds transfer fraud, other policies have modified language that may not.

Finally, often implicated exclusions in funds transfer fraud claims are funneling exclusions. These exclusions come in varying forms across different standard form policies and manuscript policies. An example of one type of funneling exclusion is as follows:

> Fraudulent Instructions
> any transfer, payment, or delivery of **Covered Property**:

17. Some insurers continue to write policies that do not contain the additional language discussed herein. Thus, this exclusion may be applicable to certain claims. It is important to thoroughly read the language of the relevant policy.
18. Commercial Crime Policy, CR 00 22 11 15 (ISO Props., Inc. 2015).

(i) approved by an **Employee**; or
(ii) arising out of any misrepresentation received by any **Employee**, agent, independent contractor, or other representative of the **Insured**,

whether such transfer, payment, or delivery was made in good faith or as a result of trick, deceit, fraud, or false pretenses, except when otherwise covered under Insuring Clauses A or E;

Other policies take a slightly different approach to funneling exclusions and may state for example, "any loss resulting, either directly or indirectly, from a forgery, is not covered under any insuring agreement other than Insuring Agreement B." While these funneling exclusions have existed for some time, they have become increasingly more common in electronic crimes, especially with respect to social engineering-based claims. These funneling exclusions, like the example above, work to limit certain types of losses to specific insuring agreements and help define the scope of coverage under commercial crime policies.

Again, while there is case law discussing these types of exclusions as they apply to other insuring agreements in commercial crime policies, there is very limited case law discussing these exclusions specifically relating to funds transfer fraud.

D. Other Claim Considerations

Just like in underwriting, the claims process has important considerations relating to technology. The most obvious is understanding the technology used to perpetrate the fraud to assist in determining whether coverage exists under the relevant policy. Some evidence and considerations face the urgency of a ticking clock. In the first hours of an investigation, there are certain items that should be prioritized including:

1. Collecting forensic evidence: Unified Audit Logs in Microsoft 365 or the Gmail Investigation Tool can reveal unauthorized sign-ins, rule changes, and OAuth grants.
2. Examining mailbox configurations: Inbox rules, delegates, and external forwarding settings often indicate persistence.
3. Collecting evidence: Collect any evidence from EDR/XDR, SEIM systems, etc. for entry points, or failed detections.

4. Reviewing email headers: SPF, DKIM, and DMARC authentication results clarify whether spoofing or compromise occurred.
5. Confirming payment settlement status: If funds moved over FedNow or RTP, recovery changes are negligible; if funds moved via ACH, return options may still exist depending on timing.

Often, insureds do not submit commercial crime claims in the first few days following their loss. In those instances, the insured may have hired a third-party, or performed certain of the tasks discussed above themselves. Claims professionals should familiarize themselves with these actions to assist in drafting requests for information that may be applicable to funds transfer fraud claims and consider whether retaining a knowledgeable professional, such as a forensic computer expert, would assist in the investigation and evaluation of the insured's claim.

VI. Conclusion

Funds transfer fraud may not be the most common type of claim seen in today's insurance landscape, but understanding the potential implications of funds transfer fraud risk and coverage is critical for insurers. Given the technical nature of funds transfer fraud claims, underwriters and claims professionals may be faced with significant challenges in trying to evaluate the risk of underwriting an insured, or in properly evaluating coverage for a claim. Even courts, though primarily dealing with computer fraud, have struggled to understand the sophisticated technology behind many electronic schemes; and have found themselves issuing conflicting decisions across different jurisdictions. Hopefully this chapter will assist underwriters and claims professionals alike in understanding some of the nuances involved with funds transfer fraud coverage, but continued education on fraudster's ever-evolving schemes will continue to be important in properly evaluating the insured's risks and claims.

CHAPTER 7

SOCIAL ENGINEERING/BUSINESS EMAIL COMPROMISE—EVOLUTION AND DEVELOPMENTS

Adam P. Friedman

I. Introduction

Thanks to the internet, for the past three decades people have had more information available to them—literally at their fingertips—than at any time in human history. Yet over the same three decades, businesses not only have continued to sustain significant losses as a result of social engineering frauds, but the magnitude of these losses, incredibly, continues to increase. According to the FBI's Internet Crime Complaint Center, 2024 was a record year for internet crime, with crimes involving phishing and spoofing of e-mail addresses not only leading the pack but occurring at a rate more than twice that of internet extortion, which is second on the list.[1]

One might imagine that businesses would be educating their employees about social engineering frauds and that individuals would be well aware of methods that fraudsters have been using for more than 30 years to trick them into sending their employers' money to unintended recipients. Notwithstanding the training efforts of insureds, however, fidelity and cyber insurers continue to be avalanched with claims seeking indemnity for losses resulting from employees sending substantial

1. FBI Internet Crime Complaint Center, Internet Crime Report (2024), available at https://www.ic3.gov/AnnualReport/Reports/2024_IC3Report.pdf.

amounts to a vendor's supposed "new bank account," pursuant to information provided in an e-mail from a spoofed address.

Whether much has changed on the insureds' end over the last three decades may be an open question; however, insurers have taken steps to clarify the fact that traditional fidelity coverages do not apply – and were never intended to apply – to losses resulting from social engineering fraud. Most notable has been the introduction of specific insuring agreements, typically included in riders or endorsements, adding "social engineering fraud" coverage at a sublimit that is markedly reduced from the coverage limit for more traditional coverage. The industry's efforts to confine social engineering fraud losses to an insuring agreement created specifically to address such claims with a significantly reduced sublimit, however, has met with mixed success at the courts. This chapter discusses some of these most recent decisions involving social engineering fraud claims.

II.
Traditional Coverage—Scope and History

Fidelity insurance has always been about protecting a bank or business against a loss that it could not prevent, despite commercially reasonable efforts to minimize the risk of loss. For example, coverage exists for a loss resulting from reliance upon an altered document when the insured has "actual physical possession" of the altered document itself, but coverage does not exist when the insured merely possesses a copy of the document, as an alteration is much more difficult to detect in a copy than in the original. Coverage also requires that a loss "result directly from" a covered risk, not from, for example, an employee's intervening acts or omissions.

Fidelity insurance never insured against the risk of loss resulting from all possible types of fraud that might be perpetrated upon an insured. Accordingly, as banking and commerce grew into the internet age – and fidelity coverage changed concomitantly – the industry's view was that modern social engineering frauds were no different from more traditional frauds against which fidelity did not insure; the only difference was that employees were being tricked and manipulated by e-mails instead of by paper or telephone. In fact, the concept of "social engineering"—a fraudster's use of some method to swindle and manipulate—was not new to the internet age; only the use of a computer to perpetrate the manipulation was.[2]

For reasons that can be debated, some courts did not share the industry's view of the risks against which its product insured. It also was clear that insureds believed (or purported to believe) that their fidelity coverage protected them against loss resulting from social engineering frauds that involved *any* use of a computer whatsoever. To address the apparent expectations of insureds, the risk of adverse decisions, and the continuously burgeoning number of losses insureds continue to sustain as a result of computer-based social engineering frauds, insurers introduced specific social engineering fraud coverage.

III.
The Addition of Social Engineering Coverage

As the market demanded the addition of potential coverage for social engineering fraud, insurers developed insuring agreements to address that particular risk. Usually an optional coverage added via endorsement or rider at an additional premium, the social engineering fraud coverage is provided at a significantly reduced sublimit, allowing insurers to control their own exposure to social engineering fraud loss amounts.

Of course, the introduction of this new, specific social engineering fraud coverage has not stopped insureds from claiming that a loss resulting from social engineering fraud is covered by another insuring agreement with a much higher coverage limit. While the coverage is still relatively nascent, early litigations involving such disputes resulted in decisions that indicate how courts view this new coverage and its interplay with other insuring agreements. Some of these decisions may have led to revisions in social engineering insuring agreements to address apparent judicial misinterpretations of the coverage.

A. Strict Application of the Insuring Agreement Distinctions

One of the earlier reported decisions involving a loss resulting from social engineering fraud and a policy that included a specific insuring agreement intended to address such a loss was *SJ Computers, LLC v.*

2. Scott L. Schmookler & Christopher L. Kahler, *Social Engineering: Is the Manipulation of Humans a Computer Fraud?*, 22 FID. L.J. 1, 4 (2016).

Travelers Casualty and Surety Company of America,[3] a decision that seemed to bode well for the industry. In *SJ Computers,* a fraudster pretending to be a vendor of the insured e-mailed fraudulent invoices to the insured's purchasing manager. The invoices directed that payment be made by a stated deadline via wire transfer to a bank account identified in the invoice, which differed from the vendor's true account. The fraudster then hacked into the insured's e-mail system and forwarded the invoices to the insured's CEO from the purchasing manager's e-mail account. The CEO called the vendor to confirm the change in bank account information, leaving a voicemail message when nobody answered. Having not heard back from the vendor and with the (supposed) payment deadline approaching, the CEO arranged the wire transfer. By the time the CEO realized the fraud, the fraudster had withdrawn the payment from its account.

As relevant to the case, the policy contained a "Computer Fraud" insuring agreement with a $1 million limit and a "Social Engineering Fraud" insuring agreement with a $100,000 sublimit. In addition to defining "computer fraud,"[4] the "Computer Fraud" insuring agreement provided that "computer fraud" excluded "such entry or change made by an Employee [or] Authorized Person . . . made in reliance upon any fraudulent . . . instruction." Critically, the policy also said, expressly, that "Computer Fraud" did not include "Social Engineering Fraud."[5]

> "Social engineering fraud" was defined as
>
> the intentional misleading of an Employee or Authorized Person by a natural person impersonating:
>
> (1) a Vendor, or that Vendor's attorney;
> (2) a Client, or that Client's attorney;
> (3) an Employee; or
> (4) an Authorized Person,
>
> through the use of a Communication.[6]

The policy also contained an exclusion stating that the "Computer Fraud" insuring agreement does not apply to "loss resulting from forged,

---

3. 621 F. Supp. 3d 962 (D. Minn. 2022).
4. "Computer fraud" was defined as "an intentional, unauthorized, and fraudulent entry or change of data or computer instructions directly into a Computer System." *Id.* at 965.
5. *Id.*
6. *Id.* "Communication" included an e-mail.

altered, or fraudulent . . . instructions used as source documentation to enter Electronic Data or send instructions."[7]

The insurer paid the $100,000 limit of the "Social Engineering Fraud" coverage, but the insured, enticed by the substantially higher limit available for "Computer Fraud," sought coverage under that insuring agreement. Litigation ensued, the insurer moved to dismiss, and the court granted the motion in its entirety.

The decision granting the insurer's motion to dismiss squarely rejects each argument that the insured made in an effort to shoehorn its loss into "Computer Fraud" coverage, relying largely upon the policy's unambiguous edict that "Computer Fraud" and "Social Engineering Fraud" are "mutually exclusive categories."[8] The loss was clearly the result of "Social Engineering Fraud," as defined—it resulted from "(1) the intentional misleading of an Employee (the CEO of [the insured], (2) by a natural person (the bad actor) (3) impersonating a Vendor . . . or an Employee . . . (4) through the use of a Communication (the fake invoices and emails)."[9]

The court rejected the insured's contention that a proximate cause standard should be applied to "direct loss" because doing so would lead to a loss constituting both "Computer Fraud" and "Social Engineering Fraud," which the policy did not allow.[10] It therefore rejected the insured's claim that the hacking of the e-mail system opened the door to "Computer Fraud" coverage, concluding (correctly) that hacking into the e-mail system did not "directly" cause the loss. Bolstering the decision were the exclusion and the definition of "Computer Fraud"—the court held that the loss "resulted from fraudulent instructions that its CEO used as source documentation to send instructions to [the insured's] bank to send money to the bad actor's account,"[11] which both the exclusion and the definition of "Computer Fraud" precluded from constituting "Computer Fraud."

B. Contrasting Approaches with Disregard for Distinctions

One of the reasons why *SJ Computers* seemed to be a good sign for the industry is that it followed on the heels of two unfavorable decisions.

---

7. *Id.* at 970.
8. *Id.* at 969.
9. *Id.* at 970.
10. *Id.* at 968.
11. *Id.* (quotation modified).

Eight months earlier, in *Ernst & Haas Management Co. v. Hiscox, Inc.*,[12] the Ninth Circuit reversed an order that granted the insurer's motion to dismiss a claim arising from a social engineering loss that was asserted against the "Computer Fraud" and "Funds Transfer Fraud" insuring agreements in a policy that did not contain a separate "Social Engineering Fraud" insuring agreement. The facts of *Ernst & Haas* are similar to those of *SJ Computers.* A clerk of the insured received an e-mail that appeared to be from her boss, directing her to wire payment of a $50,000 invoice attached to the e-mail. She arranged the payment. She then received two additional, similar payment e-mails. She made the first payment for $100,000, but something in the second e-mail caused her to e-mail her boss, who told her that he had not requested that she make any of the prior payments. The insured sought to recover its $200,000 loss from its crime insurance policy's "Computer Fraud" and "Funds Transfer Fraud" coverages.

The "Computer Fraud" insuring agreement insured against a loss "resulting directly from the use of any computer to fraudulently cause a transfer of that property. . . ."[13] The "Funds Transfer Fraud" insuring agreement insured against a loss "resulting directly from a [Fraudulent Instruction] directing a financial institution to transfer, pay or deliver" covered property. "Fraudulent instruction" was defined to include a "written instruction initially received by You which purports to have been transmitted by an Employee but which was in fact fraudulently transmitted by someone else without Your or the Employee's knowledge or consent."[14]

Reversing the district court, the Ninth Circuit held that the "Computer Fraud" insuring agreement covered the loss because (1) the fraudster used a computer to send an e-mail and (2) the employee's transfer of money to the fraudster was "fraudulently caused" by the e-mail because she was not "*properly* authorized to pay anyone the $200,000 that [the insured] lost."[15] The latter was the Ninth Circuit's effort to harmonize the decision with its prior decision in *Pestmaster Services, Inc. v. Travelers Casualty & Surety Company of America,*[16] in which it said that "the phrase 'fraudulently

12. 23 F.4th 1195 (9th Cir. 2022).
13. *Id.* at 1198.
14. *Id.* at 1199.
15. *Id.* at 1200 (emphasis in original).
16. 656 F. App'x 332 (9th Cir. 2016).

cause a transfer' [requires] an unauthorized transfer of funds."[17] With the determination that the loss was "fraudulently caused" by the e-mails, it was not a big leap for the court to conclude that the loss resulted "directly" from the fraud, holding that the insured "immediately lost its funds when those funds were transferred . . . as directed by the fraudulent email."[18] Suggesting that the transfer was "unauthorized" because the employee was transferring funds to a fraudster, resulting in a "direct loss," seems to be a stretch—particularly where the employee did not have to seek authorization each time she was to pay an invoice – egregiously broadening the coverage from the "hacking" against which the coverage is intended to insure.

The court also reversed the dismissal of the claim against the "Funds Transfer Fraud" coverage. The district court rejected this claim because the "fraudulent instruction" did not direct a financial institution to do anything.[19] The Ninth Circuit claimed that the district court "overlook[ed] the express language of the policy, which states that funds transfer fraud includes not only fraudulent instructions sent directly to a bank, but also fraudulent instructions initially received by an employee."[20] While the court's reference to the language of the policy is correct, it then impermissibly rewrote the language of the "Funds Transfer Fraud" insuring agreement to cover a "fraudulent instruction" "that *results* in directing a financial institution to transfer funds . . .",[21] which is not what the insuring agreement provides.

Two months after *Ernst & Haas*, the District of Alaska decided *City of Unalaska v. National Union Fire Insurance Co.*,[22] in which the court granted the insured City's motion for summary judgment and denied the insurer's competing dispositive motion. The facts of *Unalaska* are, again, very similar to those of *SJ Computers*—but, unlike *Ernst & Haas*, the policy *did* include a separate social engineering fraud insuring agreement. In *Unalaska*, an accounts payable clerk of the City received an e-mail that purported to be from one of the City's vendors requesting a copy of a form to change the method of receiving payments to electronic transfers.

17. *Id.* at 333.
18. *Ernst & Haas*, 23 F.4th at 1202.
19. Ernst & Haas Mgmt. Co. v. Hiscox, Inc., No.: 20-04062, 2020 WL 6789095, *6 (C.D. Cal. Nov. 5, 2020), *rev'd*, 23 F.4th 1195 (9th Cir. 2022).
20. *Ernst & Haas*, 23 F.4th at 1202.
21. *Id.* (emphasis added).
22. 591 F. Supp. 3d 440 (D. Alaska 2022).

Subsequent e-mails submitted the form and account information, to which City employees responded, with the City eventually authorizing nearly $3 million in payments to the account of the fraudster. All but approximately $637,000 of the money was recovered.

The City asserted a claim under the "Computer Fraud" insuring agreement of its "Government Crime Policy," which had a $1 million limit. The policy also contained an "Impersonation Fraud" insuring agreement with a $100,000 sublimit. The insured paid the claim under the "Impersonation Fraud" coverage, and the City sued for the remaining $537,000 under the "Computer Fraud" insuring agreement.

The "Computer Fraud" insuring agreement covered loss "resulting directly from the use of any computer to fraudulently cause a transfer of that property from inside the 'premises' or 'banking premises' . . . to a person (other than a messenger) outside those 'premises' or . . . to a place outside those 'premises.'"[23] The "Impersonation Fraud" insuring agreement (which constituted an amendment to the "Funds Transfer Fraud" insuring agreement) added coverage for a loss

> resulting directly from a 'fraudulent instruction' directing a financial institution to transfer, pay or deliver 'funds' from your 'transfer account.' . . . [W]e will also pay for the loss of 'funds' resulting from your receipt of a 'fraudulent instruction' from a purported vendor, which advises you that the vendor's bank account information has been changed and you suffer a loss of 'funds.'[24]

Unlike *SJ Computers,* however, the policy in *Unalaska* did not expressly state that "Computer Fraud" and "Impersonation Fraud" were mutually exclusive.

The *Unalaska* decision relies heavily on *Ernst & Haas,* which was decided between oral argument of the *Unalaska* appeal and the *Unalaska* decision.[25] Like *Ernst & Haas,* it held that the mere sending of an e-mail

---

23. *Id.* at 443.
24. *Id.*
25. The decision notes that "[n]either party has directed the Court's attention to the Ninth Circuit's recent decision in *Ernst & Haas,* which was published after briefing and oral argument on the instant motions" (*id.* at 450) but, according to the docket available on PACER, the court did not allow the parties to brief the applicability of *Ernst & Haas* to the facts presented – such as the fact that the policy in Unalaska contained a separate "Impersonation Fraud" endorsement.

impersonating a vendor satisfied the requirement of the use of a computer. And using a proximate cause standard, it held that the loss, which resulted from the employee's issuance of payments to the fraudster based entirely upon e-mail communications, "resulted directly from" the fraudster's use of a computer—straying far from the idea that fidelity insurance is not intended to protect an insured against its own bad business practices.[26]

The most exasperating part of the decision, however, is the court's refusal to recognize the distinction between the coverage provided by the "Computer Fraud" insuring agreement and that provided by the "Impersonation Fraud" insuring agreement, describing such an analysis to be "precisely the kind of painstaking study of policy provisions that the Alaska Supreme Court eschews when gauging an insured's reasonable expectations of coverage."[27] In most jurisdictions, this kind of analysis—ascertaining the parties' intention through an analysis of the terms of the policy—is considered basic contract interpretation.[28]

Two years after *SJ Computers,* its luster was dimmed somewhat when the same judge decided *Interstate Removal, LLC v. National Specialty Insurance Co.,* [29] a case that involved a cyber insurance policy with a social engineering fraud endorsement. In *Interstate Removal,* a vendor of the insured sent a (legitimate) e-mail to an employee of the insured, seeking payment for vehicles that the insured purchased. An exchange of e-mails (again legitimate) culminated in the vendor providing wire transfer information. At this point, a fraudster gained access to the insured's e-mail system, read the e-mail exchanges with the vendor, and sent the employee an e-mail that appeared to be from the vendor providing "updated bank account" information. The employee wired the payment to this new

---

26. *See, e.g.*, Republic Nat'l Bank of Miami v. Fid. & Deposit Co. of Md., 894 F.2d 1255, 1263 (11th Cir. 1990) ("a banker's blanket bond is not a policy of credit insurance and does not protect the bank when it simply makes a bad business deal"); Nat'l City Bank of Minneapolis v. St. Paul Fire & Marine Ins. Co., 447 N.W.2d 171, 177 (Minn. 1989) ("The Bankers Blanket Bond is designed to protect a bank against risks of dishonesty, both external and internal, but does not insured good management nor against the risk of loss inherent in the banking operations").
27. *Unalaska*, 591 F. Supp. 3d at 451.
28. *See, e.g.*, Time Inc. v. Mut. Ins. Co., 667 F. Supp. 3d 61, 67 (S.D.N.Y. 2023) ("It is axiomatic that a contract is to be interpreted so as to give effect to the intention of the parties as expressed in the unequivocal language employed").
29. No. 23-CV-0510, 2024 Wl 1332006 (D. Minn. Mar. 28, 2024).

account. A week later, the fraudster, impersonating the insured's employee, sent an e-mail to the insured's bank, purporting to direct it to make another wire transfer. At this point, the insured learned that it had been defrauded.[30]

The insured sought coverage under both its "Computer and Funds Transfer Fraud" coverage endorsement and its "Social Engineering" coverage endorsement. The court ultimately granted the insurer's motion for summary judgment, but the decision is problematic in that, seemingly unnecessarily, it chipped away at *SJ Computers.* The court held that the loss was not covered by the "Social Engineering" coverage because the insured failed to satisfy a condition precedent to coverage (discussed further below). But the court held that the loss—a clear "Social Engineering" type of fraud—*did* constitute "Computer and Funds Transfer Fraud."

The policy defined "Computer and Funds Transfer Fraud" coverage to cover:

> a. Loss resulting directly from a fraudulent:
> (1) Entry of Electronic Data or Computer System into; or
> (2) Change of Electronic Data or Computer System within;
>
> a Computer System, provided the fraudulent entry or fraudulent change causes, with regard to Paragraphs 1.a.(1) and 1.a.(2):
> (a) Money, securities or other property to be transferred, paid or delivered; or
> (b) Your account at a financial institution to be debited or deleted.[31]

The Endorsement excluded "Loss resulting from . . . [a]n Employee or financial institute acting upon any instruction to: (1) Transfer, pay or deliver money . . . or (2) Debit or delete your account; which instruction proves to be fraudulent. . . . ."[32]

Like *Ernst & Haas* and *Unalaska,* the court held that the loss "was proximately caused by a fraudulent entry of data into [the insured's] computer system that resulted in money being transferred from [the

30. The decision does not explain how the insured learned that it had been defrauded.
31. *Id.* at *2.
32. *Id.*

insured's] bank account."[33] The court appears to have relied significantly upon the fact that, unlike the policy in *SJ Computers,* "the Court is not confronted with a policy that defines social engineering and computer fraud to be mutually exclusive. . . ."[34] But the endorsement contains an exclusion that clearly eliminates a social engineering-type of loss from coverage—and the court ultimately held that this exclusion barred coverage for the loss under the "Computer and Funds Transfer Fraud" endorsement.[35] Why the court felt the need to distinguish *SJ Computers* when the policies in the two cases are not meaningfully dissimilar is unclear and, again, disappointing.

Interstate Removal also is noteworthy because it reflects an apparent evolution in the contents of the additional social engineering fraud coverage. The policy's "Social Engineering" endorsement did not simply provide coverage for a loss resulting from a social engineering fraud at a substantially reduced sublimit; it also included, as an express condition precedent to coverage, that "the Insured's established and documented verification procedure must have been followed before acting upon" the fraudulent instruction.[36] This addition is a marked difference from the policy language involved in *Unalaska,* for example, where the City's employee did not do anything to verify the legitimacy of the e-mails or the information contained in them. And, as stated above, the claim against the "Social Engineering" endorsement failed because the insured *could not establish* that it followed a *documented* verification procedure.[37]

C. Continuing Developments

The "Social Engineering" endorsement in the cyber policy at issue in *Abraham Linc Corp. v. Spinnaker Insurance Co.*[38] contained a similar condition precedent. Although the "Social Engineering" endorsement in *Abraham Linc* did not expressly say that "Social Engineering" and "Computer and Funds Transfer Fraud" were mutually exclusive, this court

---

33. *Id.* at *4.
34. *Id.* at *3.
35. *Id.*
36. *Id.* at *5.
37. *Id.* The Endorsement also excluded loss that resulted from a hacking, which the court also found to apply, as the Amended Complaint alleged that the fraudster hacked into its e-mail system.
38. No 23-CV-98, 2024 WL 3433661 (N.D. W. Va. July 16, 2024).

followed the line of cases holding that social engineering fraud is not computer fraud or funds transfer fraud.[39]

In *Abraham Linc,* the insured made an ACH transfer to a vendor pursuant to instructions contained in an e-mail that purported to be from the vendor's representative. But the vendor's e-mail system had been hacked by an unknown third party, and the ACH transfer had been sent to an account maintained not by the vendor but by the fraudster.

The insured asserted a claim against the "Computer and Funds Transfer Fraud" coverage of its cyber policy, which had a $2 million coverage limit. This insuring agreement covered

> i. Loss resulting directly from a fraudulent:
> 1. Entry of Electronic Data or Computer System into;
> or
> 2. Change of Electronic Data or Computer System within
>
> a Computer System, by a person or organization without authorization to access such Computer System, provided the fraudulent entry or fraudulent change causes, with regard to Paragraphs a.i.(1) and a.i.(2):
> a. Your money, securities or other property to be transferred, paid or delivered; or
> b. Your account at a financial institution to be debited or deleted, or
>
> ii. Loss resulting directly from a Fraudulent Instruction directing a financial institution to debit your Transfer Account and transfer, pay or deliver money or securities from that account . . . .[40]

The policy also contained a "Social Engineering" endorsement, with a $100,000 coverage sublimit, which covered loss resulting from

> the intentional misleading of an Insured to transfer Money to a person, place or account beyond the Named Insured's control resulting directly from the Named Insured's employee's good faith reliance upon an instruction transmitted via email, purporting to be from:

---

39. *See, e.g.*, Miss. Silicon Holdings, L.L.C. v. Axis Ins. Co., 843 F. App'x 581 (5th Cir. 2021); Universal Am. Corp. v. Nat'l Union Fire Ins. Co. of Pittsburgh, Pa., 37 N.E.3d 78 (2015).

40. *Abraham Linc*, 2024 WL 3433661, at *2.

> i. a natural person or entity who exchanges, or is under contract to exchange, goods or services with the Named Insured for a fee (other than a financial institution, asset manager, broker-dealer, armored motor vehicle "named insured" or any similar entity); or
>
> ii. an employee of the Named Insured;
>
> but which contained a fraudulent and material misrepresentation and was sent by an imposter. As a condition precedent to coverage, the Insured's established and documented verification procedure must have been followed before acting upon such instruction.[41]

The insurer denied the claim against both the "Computer and Funds Transfer Fraud" coverage and the "Social Engineering" coverage—the latter because the insurer did not believe that the insured demonstrated compliance with an "established and documented verification procedure." Litigation ensued, and the insurer moved to dismiss.

The court granted the motion as to the "Computer and Funds Transfer Fraud" coverage. It held that this coverage required "fraudulent access" to a computer system, not a loss resulting "from content submitted by authorized users."[42] Notably, the coverage in *Abraham Linc* required that the person inputting information into the computer system be "without authorization *to access*" the computer system—language that is not present in the social engineering coverages in the decisions discussed above. Because the insured admitted "that its employees, with authorized access, initiated the ACH transfers to the fraudsters, [the insured's] computer system was not hacked and there was no unauthorized access to its computer system to warrant coverage. . . ."[43]

The court concluded that "the mere receipt of an email" was not "unauthorized access" to the insured's computer system; "without its employees inputting the fraudulent information and initiating the transfer, there would not have been a loss."[44] While this statement sounds like the rejection of a "proximate cause" standard for direct loss, the court explained that its conclusion was based not upon the meaning of "results directly from" but upon the endorsement's requirement that the person

---

41. *Id.* at *1.
42. *Id.* at *4 (citation omitted).
43. *Id.* at *5.
44. *Id.*

entering the information be "without authorization to access" the computer system.[45]

The court denied the motion to dismiss as to the "Social Engineering" endorsement, holding that the insured adequately pleaded compliance with the endorsement's condition precedent and that there was a disputed factual issue as to whether the condition precedent actually had been satisfied.[46]

Very recently, in *Blue Compass RV, LLC v. Twin City Fire Insurance Co.,* a federal court in Texas, confronted with policy language similar to that in *SJ Computers,* reached a conclusion similar to the court's conclusion in that case.[47] The insured received an e-mail from a vendor stating that the vendor was changing its banking information for payments. After a subsequent exchange of e-mails, the insured updated the vendor's banking information and wired a payment of $1.25 million. Of course, the payment went not to the vendor's account but to the account of an unknown third party.

In addition to common insuring agreements found in commercial crime policies, each of which had a $2 million coverage limit, the insured's policy included a "Deception Fraud" insuring agreement, with a $100,000 coverage sublimit. "Deception Fraud" was defined as "the intentional misleading of a person to induce the Insured to part with Money or Securities by someone, other than an identified Employee, pretending to be an Employee, owner of the Insured, or . . . (1) A Vendor; (2) A Customer; (3) A Custodian; or (4) A Messenger."[48] The policy also specifically excluded a loss resulting from "Deception Fraud" from coverage under all other insuring agreements:

> Deception Fraud Exclusions
> (1) Loss or damage resulting directly or indirectly from Deception Fraud. This exclusion shall not apply to the Deception Fraud Insuring Agreement.
> (2) Loss or damage:
> (a) resulting from Theft by an Employee;
> (b) resulting from Forgery . . .

---

45. *Id.*
46. *Id.* at *7.
47. Blue Compass RV, LLC v. Twin City Fire Ins. Co., No. 3:24-CV-1987-B, 2025 WL 1908395 (N.D. Tex. July 10, 2025).
48. *Id.* at 3.

> (c) directly related to the use of any computer to fraudulently cause a transfer of Money or Securities from inside the Premises or Banking Premises;
> (d) resulting from Funds Transfer Fraud; . . .
>
> This exclusion shall apply only to the Deception Fraud Insuring Agreement.[49]

The insurer paid the $100,000 "Deception Fraud" sublimit and the insured sued, seeking to recover under insuring agreements with a $2 million limit. The court's decision to grant the insurer's motion to dismiss seemed to be an easy one: the decision does not even discuss the substance of any other insuring agreement, focusing solely upon the language of the "Deception Fraud" insuring agreement and the fact that the policy is clear that a loss that results from "Deception Fraud" can be recovered only under the "Deception Fraud" insuring agreement.[50]

Concluding that the loss resulted from "Deception Fraud" similarly seemed to have been easy for the court. The insured was intentionally misled to part with money by someone pretending to be a vendor.[51] The court rejected the argument that the fraudulent e-mails induced the insured simply to change banking information, not to part with money, finding such an argument to be "unreasonable":

> The reason the fraudster shared false payment information was to induce [the insured] to send money to an account it thought belonged to [the vendor]. Thus, the fraudster *did* induce [the insured] to take a particular course of action in which it parted with money: [the insured] changed [the vendor's] payment information, which [the insured] used to send a payment to the fraudster during its ordinary course of business.[52]

Just as this chapter was being finalized, a federal court in Washington issued a curious decision denying a cyber insurer's motion to dismiss in *Connelly Law Offices, PLLC v. Cowbell Cyber, Incr.*[53] In this case, hackers obtained unauthorized access to a law office's e-mail system. The hackers were able to obtain information about a settlement, and through fraudulent e-mails convinced an employee to wire the settlement proceeds

---

49. *Id.*
50. *Id.*
51. *Id.* at 6.
52. *Id.* at 11.
53. No. 25-cv-00302, 2025 WL 2256657 (W.D. Wa. Aug. 7, 2025).

to an account maintained by the hackers. The beneficiaries of the settlement sued the insured, which entered into a settlement agreement pursuant to which they paid the diverted amount to the beneficiaries. The insured sought recovery from the "Security Breach Liability" insuring agreement of its cyber policy, which had a $1 million limit. The policy also had a separate "Social Engineering" endorsement with a $100,000 sublimit. It provided coverage for a "Social Engineering Loss," which was defined as "the Loss of Money as a result of a Social Engineering Incident."[54] A "Social Engineering Incident" was

> the intentional misleading of an Insured to transfer Money to a person, place or account beyond the Named Insured's control resulting directly from the Named Insured's employee's good faith reliance upon an instruction transmitted via email, purporting to be from:
>
> i. a natural person or entity who exchanges, or is under contract to exchange, goods or services with the Named Insured for a fee (other than a financial institution, asset manager, broker-dealer, armored motor vehicle "named insured" or any similar entity); or
>
> ii. an employee of the Named Insured;
>
> but which contained a fraudulent and material misrepresentation and was sent by an imposter.[55]

The endorsement included the following limitation:

> The most We will pay for all Loss covered under the Social Engineering Insuring Agreement is the Social Engineering Aggregate Sublimit of Insurance, if any, shown above or in the Declarations, which are part of, and not in addition to, the Policy Aggregate Limit of Insurance. Upon exhaustion of any Aggregate Sublimit of Insurance by such payments, We will have no further obligations of liability of any kind with respect to Loss subject to such Sublimit of Insurance.[56]

The facts underlying the loss were clear "Social Engineering" fraud. But the court held that the endorsement did not apply because it covered only "the intentional misleading of an Insured to transfer Money," and the

54. *Id.* at *8.
55. *Id.*
56. Defendants' Reply in Further Support of Its Partial Motion to Dismiss Pursuant to CR 12(b)(6), Connelly Law Offices, PLLC v. Cowbell Cyber, Inc., No. 25-cv-00302 (W.D. Wa. May 12, 2025), Dkt. No. 24 at 11.

fraudulent e-mails supposedly did not cause the insured to transfer money, they caused the insured to enter into the settlement agreement with the beneficiaries, and a settlement agreement is a contract, not money.[57]

The decision completely ignores the issue of causation. It does not appear that the insurer raised the issue in its motion papers, although the issue is one that pervades fidelity claims and fidelity litigation. Here, the "Social Engineering" endorsement covered the loss of money "as a result" of a "Social Engineering Incident." The word "direct" does not appear anywhere, to modify "result" or otherwise. If a "loss resulting directly from" can be considered to mean a "loss proximately caused by" (as some jurisdictions have held), then certainly a loss that "results from" can be considered to be a "loss proximately caused by."

There should not be any reasonable dispute that the insured's loss of money here, whether paid pursuant to a settlement agreement or not, resulted "proximately" from a "Social Engineering Incident."[58] And because the loss resulted from a "Social Engineering Incident," the insurer's liability should have been capped at the $100,000 sublimit.

IV.
Conclusion

The most recent cases discussed above reflect the evolution of coverage for losses resulting from social engineering fraud. Insurers have begun to add a specific insuring agreement, usually via rider or endorsement, with a $100,000 sublimit (typically 5% or 10% of the coverage limit for the more common insuring agreements). Despite the addition of this specific coverage, some courts are still construing social

---

57. *Connelly Law Offices,* 2025 WL 2256657, at *9.

58. *See, e.g.*, 5 John A. Appleman, INSURANCE LAW & PRACTICE, § 3083 at 309-11 (1970):

> Where a peril specifically insured against sets other causes in motion which, in an unbroken sequence and connection between the act and final loss, produces the result for which recovery is sought, the insured peril is regarded as the proximate cause of the entire loss. . . . In other words, it has been held that recovery may be allowed where the insured risk was the last step in the chain of causation set in motion by an uninsured peril, or where the insured risk itself set into operation a chain of causation in which the last step may have been an excepted risk.")

engineering losses to fit within other, higher limit coverages. Many insurers thus have modified their social engineering coverage to make clear that a loss that is covered by a social engineering insuring agreement cannot be covered by any other insuring agreement. And to avoid the insuring agreement being construed as insurance against sloppy business practices, some insurers have included—as a condition precedent – the requirement that the insured follow a verification procedure that is documented, preventing an insured from claiming after the fact that certain actions constituted "verification."

CHAPTER 8

PROPERTY COVERAGE AND LOSS OF DIGITAL ASSETS—TREATMENT AND CONSIDERATIONS

Andy J. Chambers
C. Clark Hodgson, III*

I. Introduction

Today's marketplace includes a rapidly expanding array of non-tangible digital assets that, with limited exception, are not treated as covered property under the form fidelity policies insuring most governmental and commercial enterprises.

This chapter provides a working definition for "digital assets"—a term that encompasses a spectrum of novel non-tangible financial products. For further context, we will review recent developments—economic, political, and legal—that are likely to soon impact how digital assets are treated across multiple industries, including the financial lines of insurance. With this foundation, we will review the current state of law in relation to the alleged loss of digital assets under the common fidelity policy. Finally, we conclude with a summary of prudent considerations when presented with a fidelity claim involving alleged loss of digital assets.

II. Digital Assets

In the broadest sense, the term digital assets refers to any item of perceived value that does not exist in the physical form but instead is

* The authors acknowledge the contributions of Mikayla Anderson to this chapter.

electronically rendered in digital form. This broad definition includes traditional items such as digital photos, documents, and music files, and other electronically-stored content. It also encompasses contemporary digital holdings such as cryptocurrency and digital tokens.

In 2008, Bitcoin released the world's first cryptocurrency, utilizing a new technology and digital infrastructure known as blockchain. Blockchain is a decentralized, publicly distributed digital ledger that records transactions across multiple computers.[1] In the proceeding years, blockchain gained wide-spread market acceptance and was utilized to develop a multiplicity of new digital assets. The two most prevalent forms of blockchain-based digital assets are cryptocurrency, such as Bitcoin, and digital tokens, discussed below.

Cryptocurrency is commonly understood as a digital form of money. However, unlike physical money, cryptocurrencies are not created or issued by governments or other financial institutions, but instead are created and secured online by private parties though cryptographic algorithms, within a decentralized network of computers that validate and maintain the transaction ledger. Perhaps the best-known cryptocurrency is Bitcoin, which has a fixed and limited supply of coins, may be used as a medium of exchange, and is supported by generally accepted blockchain technology. Based on these characteristics, Bitcoin and other similar forms of cryptocurrency are perceived to have inherent value with clear market utility.[2]

Tokens are digital assets that represent a specific value, utility, or right within a particular blockchain ecosystem. Digital tokens may be fungible (i.e., interchangeable) or nonfungible (i.e., unique). Nonfungible tokens (NFTs) represent ownership to a specific item of digital art or other content. NFTs are not interchangeable, as each one is unique. Fungible tokens are like cryptocurrencies in that they may be used as a store of value

---

1. Report of the President's Working Group on Digital Asset Markets, *supra* note 2, pg. 15, *citing* Satoshi Nakamoto, Bitcoin: A Peer-to-Peer Electronic Cash System (Oct. 31, 2008).
2. In contrast, some forms of digital assets, such as meme coins, do not have inherent value or any clear utility. Meme coins are a form of cryptocurrency inspired by social, cultural, and political trends, often created for entertainment or satirical purposes, without a robust technological foundation or real-world utility.

and medium for exchange. In addition, fungible tokens may be used in connection with a variety of other non-monetary legal interests.[3]

Given the market success and sweeping application of blockchain technology, traditional forms of digital property that do not rely on blockchain are properly viewed as a distinct form of digital asset, with diminishing market relevance. Indeed, the most recent definition provided by the U.S. executive administration defines digital assets in a manner that is limited to blockchain-based assets, excluding traditional forms of non-blockchain digital property.[4]

III.
The Shifting Economic, Political, and Legal Landscape

In the less than twenty (20) years since Bitcoin was introduced, the global market for cryptocurrency ballooned from $0 to nearly $4 Trillion,[5] with annual revenue projected to exceed $100 Billion in 2025.[6] Similarly, the tokenization of real-world assets continues at rapid pace and is

---

3. Fungible tokens include: (a) stablecoins—digital tokens akin to cryptocurrency designed to maintain a stable value relative to an asset such as the US dollar or commodities such gold); (b) asset-backed tokens—digital tokens that represent real-world assets like real estate or commodities, allowing fractional ownership and increased liquidity; (c) security tokens—digital tokens used to represent ownership or rights to assets, such as company shares; (d) governance tokens—digital tokens that grant the holder voting power within a decentralized organization or project; and (e) decentralized finance (DeFi) tokens—digital tokens granting access to peer-to-peer financial services, supported by blockchain ledger system, without the need for traditional intermediaries.
4. Executive Order No. 14178, Strengthening American Leadership in Digital Financial Technology, 90 Fed. Reg. 8647 §§ 1, 4 (Jan. 31, 2025); *See also*, Report of the President's Working Group on Digital Asset Markets, pg. 15 (Jul. 30, 2025)(defining digital assets as any digital representation of value that is record on a distributed ledger through blockchain technology), available at www.whitehouse.gov/crypto/ (Aug. 4, 2025).
5. https://www.coingecko.com/en/global-charts (Aug. 4, 2025).
6. Digital Assets—Worldwide, Statista Market Insights (May 2025), available at www.statista.com/outlook/fmo/digital-assets/worldwide (Aug. 4, 2025).

expected to reach $600 Billion in assets under management by 2030.[7] The trajectory of current economic forces suggest robust expansion and integration of digital assets across financial markets.

At the same time, governments around the world are increasingly focused on how to treat, promote, and regulate the emerging markets in digital assets. This is certainly true in the United States, where in 2025 alone there have been numerous political developments certain to impact the future treatment of digital assets. Among other important developments, the Executive Administration started the year with Executive Order No. 14178, Strengthening American Leadership in Digital Financial Technology, offered in support of the administration's stated goal to make the United States the "crypto capital of the world."[8] Relatedly, in July 2025, Congress passed, and the President signed into law, the GENIUS Act, creating the first-ever federal regulatory framework for stablecoins.[9] The current political environment in the United States appears to be ripe for new regulations to both govern and promote the development of an "on-chain" digitized financial system.

There have been developments on the legal front as well. In a series of recent cases, the courts have, for the first time, been forced to address various challenges related to cryptocurrency and its regulatory implications. The common inquiry is whether cryptocurrency qualifies as (1) a commodity subject to regulatory oversight and enforcement by the Commodity Futures Trading Commission (CFTC), (2) a security subject to regulatory oversight and enforcement by the Securities Exchange Commission (SEC), (3) both a commodity and security, subject to the jurisdiction of both the CFTC and the SEC, or (4) none of the above. Of the numerous cases filed by regulators, many were ultimately withdrawn, settled, or otherwise dismissed without a final decision or other resulting

---

7. Tokenized Funds: The Third Revolution in Asset Management Decoded, Boston Consulting Group (October 2024), available at https://web-assets.bcg.com (Aug. 4, 2025).
8. *Supra* note 5.
9. S.1582 - GENIUS Act, available at www.congress.gov; *See also*, Report of the President's Working Group on Digital Asset Markets (Jul. 30, 2025), *supra* note 5; Public Statement by Paul S. Atkins, Chairman of the Securities and Exchange Committee, titled American Leadership in the Digital Finance Revolution (July 31, 2025), available at www.sec.gov.

legal precedent.[10] However, several cases were litigated, resulting in legal precedent at the federal district court level. Together, these cases suggest that cryptocurrency may, under the existing regulatory scheme, be treated as both a commodity and as a security, subject to the jurisdiction of both the CFTC and SEC.[11]

The combined weight of economic, political, and legal change underway with respect to digital assets is almost certain to impact financial crime insurance in the near term. In light of the rapid pace of change, the authors found the following resources helpful in staying abreast of current

---

10. Kentucky, et al. v. SEC, No. 3:24-cv-00069 (E.D. Ky. Nov. 14, 2024) (suit filed by 18 states to challenge the SEC's authority to regulate digital assets trading platforms as securities; case stayed by stipulation of the parties); SEC v. Coinbase, Inc., 726 F. Supp 3d 260 (S.D.N.Y. 2024) (SEC dismissed enforcement action following interlocutory appeal by Coinbase); Blockchain Ass'n et al., v. IRS, No.3:24-cv-03259-X(N.D. Tex. Dec. 27, 2024) (three blockchain industry associations filed suit challenging rule that requires certain cryptocurrency exchanges to comply with broker reporting requirements; case voluntarily dismissed by plaintiffs); Bitnomial Exchange, LLC v. SEC, No. 1:24-cv-09904 (N.D. Ill. Oct. 10, 2024) (suit challenging SEC's attempt to classify XRP futures contracts as a security; case voluntarily dismissed by plaintiff).
11. *See*, CFTC v. McDonnell, 287 F. Supp. 3d 213 (E.D.N.Y. 2018) (held that the Commodity Futures Trading Commission (CFTC) has the authority to regulate virtual currencies as commodities and to prosecute fraud related to them); CFTC v. Ikkurty, No. 1:22-cv-02465, 2024 WL 3251348 (N.D. Ill. July 1, 2024)(held that Bitcoin and Ether are commodities within the CFTC's jurisdiction); SEC v. Terraform Labs Pte. Ltd., 708 F. Supp. 3d 450 (S.D.N.Y. 2023) (held that a particular Ethereum blockchain token constituted a security subject to SEC regulation); SEC v. Ripple Labs, Inc., 682 F. Supp 3d 308 (S.D.N.Y. 2023) (held that sale of crypto currency to institutional investors constituted the sale of securities, while programmatic sales on secondary markets did not); SEC v. Coinbase, Inc., 726 F. Supp 3d 260 (S.D.N.Y. 2024)(trial court denied Coinbase's motion to dismiss, finding that the SEC's allegations regarding Coinbase's crypto transactions were sufficient to invoke SEC jurisdiction); *See also*, CFTC Office of the General Counsel, Letter at 1, SEC v. Telegram Group Inc., 448 F. Supp. 3d 352 (S.D.N.Y. 2020) ("[T]he [CEA] . . . provides that many securities are commodities to which the securities laws apply. Thus, any given digital asset may or may not be subject to the securities laws, but that does not depend on whether the asset is a commodity. It depends on whether the asset is a 'security' within the meaning of the '33 Act itself.").

developments, which may serve as a resource to claims handlers in the future, as well:

- Federal Bureau of Investigations—Cyber (https://www.fbi.gov/investigate/cyber);
- Federal Trade Commission (https://consumer.ftc.gov);
- Commodity Futures Trading Commission: Digital Assets (https://www.cftc.gov/digitalassets/index.htm)
- U.S. Securities and Exchange Commission, Crypto Task Force (https://www.sec.gov/about/crypto-task-force);
- The White House: Crypto (https://www.whitehouse.gov/crypto/);
- CoinDesk.com (a non-governmental source of news and information about crypto currencies and blockchain technology); and
- https://www.crypto-law.us/ (U.S. Legal and Regulatory News for Digital Asset Holders)

IV.
Digital Assets Are Not Covered Under Most Form Fidelity Policies, Except By Scheduled Endorsement

With limited exception available by endorsement alone, fidelity policies generally do not cover loss of digital assets.

Prior to 2015, the form fidelity policies were silent on the matter of digital assets. Nonetheless, digital assets arguably have always been outside of coverage under the common fidelity policies as a matter of definition. Fidelity policies extend coverage to the loss of three defined categories of property: “money”, “securities”, and “other property”. The same is true under the Standard Form 24 Fidelity Bond.

“Money” is generally defined as cash or other recognized currency having a face value. Digital assets are not a form of recognized currency with a static face value and, therefore, cannot be considered “money.” “Securities” are defined as negotiable and nonnegotiable instruments or contracts representing money or property (i.e., investment contracts). Prior to the *Ripple* decision issued by the Southern District of New York in July 2023, digital assets were generally considered to be something other than securities, and there was no case precedent to suggest otherwise. Accordingly, digital assets have typically been viewed as something other than securities for purposes of the fidelity policy. Lastly, “other property” is generally defined as tangible property other than money or securities that has intrinsic value. While certain digital assets may have intrinsic value, digital assets are not tangible and, therefore, do not qualify as "other property."[12] Digital assets do not, as a matter of definition, qualify as any one of these three categories of covered property. As a result, the loss of digital assets is not a covered peril under the fidelity policy.

In 2015, ISO introduced a new set of fidelity forms that explicitly excluded coverage for all forms of "virtual currencies". For example, the

---

12. *See generally*, Sedaghatpour v. Lemonade Ins. Co., No. 1:22-cv-00355, 2024 WL 4563855, at *1 (4th Cir. Oct. 24, 2024) (theft of cryptocurrency did constitute a direct physical loss as necessary to implicate coverage under homeowner's policy and, therefore, was not subject to coverage); Rosenberg v. Homesite Ins. Agency, Inc., 683 F. Supp. 3d 926 (D. Minn. 2023) (theft of cryptocurrency tokens was not "direct physical loss" to property under the policy's theft coverage); Burt v. Travelers Com. Ins. Co., 621 F. Supp. 3d 1049, 1052 (N.D. Cal. 2022) (theft of cryptocurrency was not a "direct physical loss" because cryptocurrency does not have a "material existence, formed out of tangible matter, [nor] is [it] perceptible to the sense of touch."); Kem Krest LLC v. Hanover Ins. Co., No. 3:21-CV-572 RLM-MGG, 2023 WL 1795879 (N.D. Ind. Feb. 6, 2023) (electronic transfer is not transfer of currency, coin or bank note; money applies to physical, tangible money); Ox Labs Inc. v. BitPay, Inc., 848 F. App'x 795 (9th Cir. 2021)(in a conversion action to recover Bitcoins, court concluded that specific recovery is unavailable when the converted property is intangible); Ward Gen. Ins. Servs., Inc. v. Emps. Fire Ins. Co., 114 Cal. App. 4th 548, 7 Cal. Rptr. 3d 844 (2003), as modified on denial of reh'g (Jan. 7, 2004) (holding that data was not tangible property covered by property policy); but see, NMS Servs. Inc. v. Hartford, 62 F. App'x 511 (4th Cir. 2003) (deleted files necessary for operation of insured's computer network result in actual physical damage, implicating potential coverage under property policy); Caroln Co. v. Delaget, LLC, No. 11-CV-477-JPS, 2012 WL 1854146 (W.D. Wis. May 21, 2012) (suggested that the term "money" might, in certain circumstances, include electronic money); Synnex Corp. v. Axis Ins. Co., No. 4:20-CV-07244-YGR, 2023 WL 2530930 (N.D. Cal. Mar. 15, 2023)(loss of software installed on insured's network constituted "other property" subject to coverage under property policy). Importantly, the above line of cases all involved property policies. In contrast to the common property policy, most modern fidelity policies expressly exclude from coverage loss of computer programs and electronic data.

2015 Commercial Crime Policy includes the following exclusion for loss of virtual currency:

> This Policy does not cover:
>
> **k. Virtual Currency**
>
> Loss involving virtual currency of any kind, by whatever name known, whether actual or fictious, including, but not limited to, digital currency, crypto currency or any other type of electronic currency.[13]

While digital assets do not satisfy the definitions of money, securities, or other property, addition of the exclusion solidifies the notion that digital assets are not covered property. The added exclusion for virtual currency under the updated ISO crime and theft forms or similar iterations is now commonplace in the market.

Contemporaneous with ISO's release of the updated 2015 fidelity forms, ISO released a new "Virtual Currency as Money" endorsement, with a revised definition of money to include scheduled virtual currency, subject to a sublimit.[14] To qualify for the endorsement, the virtual currency must be one that is traded on a recognized exchange and identified in the schedule on the face of the endorsement. Coverage under the endorsement is subject to a sublimit, to be determined in underwriting and included in the schedule on the face of the endorsement. Valuation for loss of virtual currency under the endorsement is based on the "value at the close of business on the day the loss was 'discovered' as determined by the rate of exchange published by the Exchange shown in the schedule." Lastly, the 2015 endorsement provides the insurance company with the option to settle and pay any loss in the same virtual currency or its U.S. dollar equivalent.

---

13. ISO CR 0022 11 15.
14. *See*, ISO form endorsements CR 25 45 (applies to the employee theft insuring agreement or the computer and funds transfer fraud agreement, or to both) and CR 25 46 (applies to the employee theft insuring agreement alone).

V.
Claim Review Considerations

The loss of digital assets implicates a relatively narrow claim analysis under current form fidelity policies because such policies do not cover digital assets, except by scheduled endorsement. As a result, an initial review of the policy, supported by an adequate understanding of the claim presented, may be dispositive. If the loss involves digital assets but the policy does not include an endorsement for virtual currencies, the traditional fidelity policy will not respond. Alternatively, to the extent the policy includes an endorsement for virtual currencies, the claim review will be limited by the conditions, elements, and sub-limits stated on the face of the endorsement. In this context there are several important issues to consider.

As a starting point, the endorsement for virtual currency as money is offered only for insurer-approved forms of currency traded within a recognized exchange system. Both the name of the currency and the name of the exchange must be listed in the schedule to the endorsement. Coverage under the endorsement is strictly limited to named virtual currency. Conversely, the endorsement does not cover digital assets that are not identified in the schedule. By limiting coverage to virtual currencies traded within approved exchange systems, the endorsement mitigates potentially difficult issues involving proof of ownership, proof of loss, and value of loss at the time of discovery.

Discovery is an item that warrants special consideration under the virtual currency endorsement. To the extent coverage may be afforded for loss of digital currency, the value of the covered loss is to be determined as of the date of discovery, not the date of transfer. This is important because virtual currency markets are notoriously volatile, with the potential for material changes in value day-to-day. Further, while the date of transfer is a knowable fact, the discovery analysis involves certain subjective elements that may allow for differing views as to when the circumstances culminated to actual discovery of loss. These policy dynamics may, under certain scenarios, create financial incentives for the insured to incline towards a more advantageous discovery date associated with a higher daily value. For these reasons, discovery warrants special attention early in the claim review and may require a fact-intensive investigation to include interviews of those individuals involved in discovering the loss and requests for other reliable evidence to substantiate the reported discovery date.

Unlike the common fidelity claim, a claim made under the virtual currency endorsement necessitates a tiered, two-part claim analysis. The endorsement is not a stand-alone insuring agreement, meaning that it does not create a new covered cause of loss. Rather, the endorsement creates a sublimit of coverage under the employee theft insuring agreement or the computer and funds transfer fraud insuring agreement. To qualify for coverage under the endorsement, the insured must first establish a covered cause under one of these two insuring agreements, requiring a second-level of analysis and substantiation not present in the traditional claim.

Relatedly, the nature of virtual currency may create special challenges for the insured with respect to its duty to substantiate the underlying cause of loss. The anonymized blockchain environment obscures most everything except that which is necessary to fulfill the ledger requirements. This practical reality can make it difficult to determine the most basic coverage questions, such as what happened, why it happened, and who was responsible. This is an area where the claims handler might consider retaining the services of an expert consultant specializing in blockchain and cybersecurity forensics, in order to acquire the universe of relevant information and determine what might reasonably be inferred therefrom.

Lastly, as with any other claim, it is important to consider whether the circumstances of the claim implicate any of the policy exclusions. In particular, loss of virtual currency may suggest consideration of exclusions for, among others, inventory loss, voluntary transfer, and fraudulent impersonation.

The following is offered as a checklist of suggested inquiries and considerations when examining a fidelity claim involving loss of digital assets:

1. Confirm the basis for the claim and obtain supporting information from the insured:
    a. What type of digital asset?
    b. When, how, and by whom was the loss discovered?
    c. What evidence is there to demonstrate:
        i. the fact, extent, ownership, and value of the digital asset at the time of the loss event?
        ii. the insured's actual, pecuniary loss of those assets?

   d. How was the claimed loss amount quantified?
   e. Under which coverage grant does the insured seek coverage: employee theft or computer and funds transfer fraud?
   f. Is there evidence to demonstrate how the loss was perpetrated?
   g. Is there evidence about the identity of the person or persons responsible for the loss?
   h. Is there sufficient information to establish a covered cause of loss under the employee theft or computer and funds transfer fraud agreement.
   i. Following discovery, what did the insured do to recover or mitigate the loss?
   j. Did the insured report the loss to law enforcement?
2. Consider whether additional investigation is warranted to determine appropriate discovery, given the relationship between discovery and valuation.
3. Identify the applicable policy period, based on the date of discovery, and conduct review to confirm presence of standard policy exclusion for loss of virtual currencies.
4. Review schedule of endorsements to identify or confirm the absence of an endorsement treating virtual currency as money.
5. If the policy includes endorsement treating virtual currency as money:
   a. Identify the scheduled sublimit of insurance.
   b. Identify the name of the virtual currency to which the endorsement extends coverage.
   c. Identify the virtual currency exchange listed in the endorsement schedule.
   d. Identify the available insuring agreement(s) to which the endorsement is attached: employee theft, computer and funds transfer fraud, or both?
   e. Determine whether there is sufficient evidence to establish a covered cause of loss under one of the two insuring agreements.
6. Consider consulting with specialized consultants in the areas of:
   a. Blockchain forensics—for purposes of tracing stolen assets.
   b. Cybersecurity forensics—for purposes of determining the cause of loss.

7. Consider requesting crypto-specific information and records, that might include:
    a. A statement from the insured about the lost virtual assets and the private key associated therewith:
        i. When was the key acquired?
        ii. When was the private key lost?
        iii. Circumstances surrounding lost key: Who had control? What type of hardware utilized to store the digital wallet?
        iv. Initial cost to the insured to acquire the crypto asset?
        v. Value of the asset when the private key was lost?
        vi. Value of the asset at the time the loss was discovered.
        vii. Basis for the insured's method of valuation?
    b. Records kept by the exchange system on which the currency is traded, to verify the insured's legal interest in the assets prior to the loss event, and the actual loss event itself, to include:
        i. Transaction IDs;
        ii. Digital wallet addresses; and
        iii. Transaction history ledger, with timestamps.
8. Consider application of policy exclusions including, among others, inventory loss, voluntary transfer, and fraudulent impersonation.

VI.
Conclusion

As the landscape of digital assets continues its course of rapid change, claims professionals must stay abreast of the developments and adapt claim handling practices accordingly. While the foregoing is not meant to be exhaustive, the authors hope it may serve as a resource to guide further consideration.

CHAPTER 9

EMERGING TECHNOLOGY SCHEMES—A CLAIM PRIMER

Iga Todd

I. Introduction

This chapter provides a brief overview of various fidelity/crime coverages, the common coverage issues requiring examination, and recent examples of claims that demonstrate how technology plays a role in the way various losses occur.

II. Employee Theft/Dishonesty

A. Coverage Issues for Employee Theft/Dishonesty Claims

A central issue in any employee theft/dishonesty claim is whether the alleged bad actor qualifies as an "employee" under the Policy. Claims professionals should request a personnel file. While W2 employees, volunteers, leased/seasonal and temporary employees generally satisfy the definition, an issue often arises for individuals issued a 1099. Some policies exclude independent contractors from the definition of "employee," while other policies may add coverage for such individuals through endorsement. Moreover, as some entities share employees across organizational lines, issues may arise regarding whether an individual is an employee of an insured entity. Careful consideration of the definition, and any endorsed amendments, is critical.

Whether a claim evidences "theft" or dishonesty may also require close examination. Theft requires an intentional unlawful taking of "money," "securities" or "other property." Many policies require an intentional and unlawful taking to the deprivation of the insured, while others are silent on the requirement of intent. While dishonesty is not a defined term, many policies require the employee act dishonestly or fraudulently with the manifest intent to cause the insured to sustain a loss and/or obtain a financial benefit. Most commercial crime policies provide coverage for loss caused by employee theft as opposed to employee dishonesty.

Finally, a frequent issue arises with respect to the requirement that an insured sustain a direct loss as a result of employee theft/dishonesty in circumstances in which the insured settles its liability to a third party caused by the conduct of its employee. For example, an employee of the insured may abuse his or her position to steal from a third-party customer. In those circumstances, the insured's election to make its customer whole is not a direct loss covered by the policy. However, some policies now include additional endorsements providing coverage for loss to a client caused by an employee.

B. Illustrative Cases

1. Who is an "Employee"?

An individual employed by a parent company handled financial matters for both the parent and its subsidiaries. The insured submitted a claim alleging the individual stole from the insured subsidiary; however, the parent company—not an insured—issued his paycheck. The policy defined employee to mean an individual "whom you compensate directly by salary, wages or commissions. . . ." Therefore, the court found he was not an employee of the insured subsidiary to trigger coverage under the policy.[1]

The insured and an individual changed their working relationship in an employment contract by adding an addendum converting the individual from an employee to an independent contractor. Thereunder, the individual's tax treatment changed, despite continuing obligations to the

1. T.S.I. Holdings, Inc. v. Buckingham, 885 F. Supp. 1457 (D. Kan. 1995).

insured. The court held that the insured was unable—given the agreement—to establish the individual was an employee at the time of loss, given the definition of "employee" excluded independent contractors.[2]

The insured submitted a claim for employee theft by an individual who worked out of the insured's corporate office, received health benefits, and held himself out to the public as an employee of the insured. Finding the individual satisfied the definition of "employee" in the policy, the court agreed with the insured that it demonstrated its right to control the individual, even where actual control was absent.[3]

2. Is There "Theft" or Dishonesty?

An employee in the insured's credit department forged signatures on letters of credit to make it appear that a third-party buyer of fuel owned more collateral than it actually did. The Fifth Circuit held that the employee's actions did not constitute a "theft" because the dishonest employee did not exercise control over the fuel, he merely ensured that it was sold to the third party, and thus there was no "taking."[4]

An employee misrepresented to the insured the prices customers were willing to pay for corn and sorghum, which led the insured to ship additional grain sold at prices below those reflected in the insured's accounting system. The Eighth Circuit held there was a "theft," finding that while the employee never physically seized the grain, a physical seizure was not necessary because a "taking" encompasses an "implicit transfer" of control. There was an unlawful taking because the employee "took implicit control over the grain" and "exercised her authority to direct the transfer and sale of the grain."[5]

A board member who had influence over which properties the insured purchased recommended that the insured purchase properties in which he had a financial interest without disclosing his interests. When the insured found out, it argued that it could have purchased these properties at a much

---

2. Mgmt. Recruiters v. Travelers Indem. Co. of Am., No. 2:13-cv-2001, 2014 WL 201070 (W.D. Pa. 2014).
3. In re Baker & Getty Fin. Servs., Inc., 93 B.R. 559 (Bankr. N.D. Ohio 1988).
4. Tesoro Ref. & Mktg. v. Nat'l Union Fire Ins. Co., 833 F.3d 470, 476-480 (5th Cir. 2016).
5. Nat'l Union Fire Ins. Co. v. Cargill, Inc., 146 F. Supp. 2d 541, 549-53 (8th Cir. 2021).

lower price and sought to recover its loss from its insurer. The Eleventh Circuit agreed with the insurer that the employee's conduct, though dishonest, was not theft because the employee had not "taken" money from his employer.[6]

Employees of a commercial landfill permitted truckers to dump debris for either no charge or a reduced charge in exchange for kickbacks. The insurer denied a claim for theft coverage for lost revenues because the revenues were never received by the insured and thus could not have been taken. In a confusing decision the court did not decide whether the lost revenues were received, but sua sponte found coverage because, although the employees did not remove anything from the landfill, there was a taking within the terms of the policy because the employees "effectively seized the landfill space," which it found to be "finite, real property" by permitting "occupation and transferring control over the property." While not reaching the legal issue concerning the lost revenues, the court held that the employees "did not have to physically possess the company's money for their act to constitute a taking, presumably of landfill space." It was sufficient that the employees allowed the "consumption of valuable landfill space without payment" which "resulted in an implicit, if not outright explicit, transfer of possession or control of the space to the deprivation of [the insured]."[7]

A bankruptcy trustee sought theft coverage for a series of allegedly dishonest loans made by the controlling shareholder and CEO of insured. Insurers argued that no "theft" had occurred because the funds lost through loans to third parties were asserted to be those of the insured's financer, obtained illegally by the employee, rather than the insured's own funds, and thus there was no "deprivation" to the insured. The court held this argument had no merit, stating that regardless of whether the funds had been obtained from the financer illegally, the insured was under the same obligation to repay them. Thus, the insured had suffered a deprivation, regardless of who had legal title to the lost funds.[8]

The insured's employee helped customers falsify credit applications to obtain cars they could not afford in exchange for kickbacks. Many of the customers defaulted on their loans, and the insured sought coverage under the employee theft provision of a commercial crime policy. The

6. Hartford Fire Ins. Co. v. Mitchell Co., 440 F. App'x 759 (11th Cir. 2011).
7. Recology Inc. v. Berkley Reg. Ins. Co., No. 4:20-CV-001150-PJH, 2023 WL 1070356, vacated, No. 20-cv-01150-PJH (N.D. Cal. Apr. 20, 2023)
8. In re Prime Comm. Corp., 187 B.R. 785 (Bankr. N.D. Ga. 1995).

court held that the employee engaged in theft because he aided the customers in unlawfully taking the vehicles from the dealership, as well as the funds loaned on the faith of the falsified credit applications. The court found the policy did not require the stolen property to be owned or possessed by the insured. Instead, it required only that the insured was "legally liable for the loss."[9]

A "Crimeguard" policy defined a covered loss as "the direct deprivation of the insured by a single act or series of related acts resulting from [the unlawful taking] of [money held by the Insured] to the deprivation of the Insured." The court held that an employee's payment of bribes in exchange for the customer's purchase of items from the insured at inflated prices, ultimately resulting in the insured having to refund profits from the transactions, did not constitute "theft."[10]

The insured's employee was a salesman responsible for collecting funds for goods sold. He pocketed some of the money that he should have remitted to the company. The court held that the employee's actions clearly met the definition of "theft."[11]

The insurance policy at issue covered loss resulting from theft but it excluded loss resulting from wrongful conversion or embezzlement. The insured had suffered a loss as a result of its employees' taking of cattle that belonged to the insured. The employees had access to the cattle and were entrusted with transporting them. But the employees sold the cattle and kept the proceeds for themselves. The insurer argued that the employees' acts constituted conversion or embezzlement but not theft. The policy did not define "theft," "wrongful conversion," or "embezzlement." The court held that the terms were ambiguous and had to be construed in favor of coverage.[12]

An employee manipulated accounts receivable to cause delinquent accounts to appear current to make herself and her department look better. As a result, the insured paid $200,000 in undeserved merit raises and

---

9. Taylor Chrysler Dodge, Inc. v. Universal Underwriters Ins. Co., No. 08 C 4522, 2009 WL 3187234 (N.D. Ill. 2009).

10. Williams Elec. Games v. Barry, No. 97 C 3743, 2001 WL 1104619, *aff'd sub nom.* Williams Elecs. Games, Inc. v. Garrity, 366 F.3d 569 (N.D. Ill. 2000).

11. Westfield Ins. Co. v. Jackson Wholesale Co., No. t:13-135-DCR, 2014 WL 104081 (E.D. Ky. 2014).

12. Meridian Citizens Mut. Ins. Co. v. Horton, No. 5:08-CV-302-KKC, 2010 WL 1253084 (E.D. Ky. 2010).

bonuses, and it was ultimately forced to write off over $5 million in accounts receivable. The court held that a "theft" had unquestionably occurred because the account manipulation was an "unlawful taking" that deprived the insured of its property. However, the lost accounts receivable were not recoverable under the policy because they were not "other property" as defined under Louisiana law.[13]

The insured was an automobile dealer that alleged that two employees committed theft when they used funds received from vehicle sales to pay current expenses rather than paying a lender, and improperly used income received after a certain date to pay expenses incurred before that date. The court held that the employees' acts did not constitute "theft" because there were no allegations that money was used for anything other than to pay legitimate debts owed by the insured.[14]

The insured's employee approved numerous inflated invoices submitted by a vendor. Insured argued that the employee benefitted by establishing a shell company to receive proceeds from the theft. The court rejected the argument that a "taking" for purposes of employee theft requires a physical act. The court agreed that "'taking,' for the purposes of employee theft, may be broadly construed and is not limited to 'hands in the till' or physical control over a specific item." Despite the absence of any possession or control over the money paid to the vendor, the court held that summary judgment was inappropriate on the issue of Employee Theft.[15]

The insured suffered a loss when its employee received kickbacks in exchange for approving bids from a vendor he knew were inflated, thus causing his employer to overpay. The court held that the part of the insured's loss that resulted from overpayments was not covered, reasoning that the policy was designed "to protect it from employee theft, not against a less favorable deal from a deceitful contractor," but found the kickbacks were covered because the insured had "intended to pay only its

---

13. Morris Kirschman & Co. v. Hartford Fire Ins. Co., No. Civ. A. 03-1743, 2004 WL 1934848 (E.D. La. 2004).
14. Coopersville Motors, Inc. v. Fed. Mut. Ins. Co., 771 F. Supp. 2d 796, 890 (W.D. Mich. 2010).
15. Sherwin-Williams Co. v. Beazley Ins. Co., No. 18-cv-02964 (DFW/DTS), 2020 WL 4226866 (D. Minn. 2020).

independent contractor for work performed, and had not authorized a payment to [the dishonest employee]."[16]

The insured automobile dealer had an employee who was engaged in two separate dishonest schemes. First, he was embezzling money from his employer by converting to his own use money orders that the employer meant for third parties. Second, he was allowing customers of the insured to purchase cars far beyond what their credit would allow by falsifying their credit applications. Many of these customers defaulted on their loans to the insured, causing it to suffer a loss. The court held that the employee's conversion of money orders constituted a theft, but that the employee's practice of falsifying credit applications did not constitute a "theft," explaining that although the employee's actions may have been dishonest, they did not constitute a "taking."[17]

Insured's employee obtained pharmaceuticals for his employer from illegal sources, and the pharmaceuticals were subsequently seized by the New York Attorney General. The insured sought recovery for employee theft. The court denied the insurer's motion to dismiss, noting that dismissals are appropriate only if the policy terms are clear and unambiguous. The court held that there were ambiguities in the policy language. With very little analysis, and no explanation of which terms were ambiguous, the court held that whether a "theft" had occurred could not be decided on a motion to dismiss because several of the key terms were open to different interpretations.[18]

The insured was hired to administer an employee benefit plan. The insured's employees had a practice of delaying payment of employee benefits as long as possible and using the funds to pay for the insured's operating expenses. No employee actually took any funds for their own use. In a poorly reasoned decision, the court held that theft was not limited to an embezzlement-like act but could instead encompass any fraudulent or dishonest criminal act. The court held that when the insured exercised

---

16. Frazier Indus. Co. v. Navigators Ins. Co., 149 F. Supp. 3d 512, 519 (D.N.J. 2015).
17. Pine Belt Auto. v. Royal Indem. Co., No. 06-5995 (JAP), 2008 WL 4682582 (D.N.J. 2008), *aff'd*, 400 F. App'x 621 (3d Cir. 2010), *and aff'd*, 400 F. App'x 621 (3d Cir. 2010).
18. Allion Healthcare, Inc. v. Arch Ins. Co., No. CV 14-0147, 2014 WL 4829463 (E.D.N.Y. 2014).

control over the funds without consent, it deprived the insured of the funds for immediate payment, which constituted a theft.[19]

An employee manipulated company data to overstate profits, triggering payment of unearned bonuses to other employees. The court considered whether there was coverage under an employee theft provision. The court concluded the dishonest employee's conduct was "theft" within the meaning of the policy even where the employee did not herself possess the company's losses. There was coverage notwithstanding that the employee's chosen method of separating the insured from its money incidentally benefitted third parties, and the employee's benefit was disproportionate to the insured's loss. The court noted that "the insurer promised to cover [the insured's] loss, however, not the employee's gain."[20]

The principal violated the insured's trading program guidelines by accident, and the insured suffered significant losses as a result. To cover up his mistake, the principal continued to violate the guidelines in the hopes that he would avoid having to confess his error. The court found that the principal did not intend to deprive the insured of its money, but was hoping to recoup the losses he negligently caused. The employee lacked intent to defraud the insured. The court held that no "taking" occurred because the principal had merely gambled with the insured's money in the hopes of winning it back.[21]

The improper use of genetic information was held not to constitute a "taking" and, thus, was not a "theft." The court rejected the insured's proposed definition derived from statutory definitions of larceny because the term "theft" was unambiguous.[22]

The court found that "unlawful taking" meant that the employee had to intend to commit theft, which could not be shown by violation of company policy alone.[23]

---

19. Guyan Int'l, Inc. v. Prof'l Benefits Adm'rs, Inc., No. 5:10 CV 823, 2013 WL 1338194 (N.D. Ohio 2013).
20. Whitney Equip. Co. v. Travelers Cas. & Sur. Co. of Am., 431 F.Supp.3d 1223 (W.D. Wash. 2020).
21. Apollo Computer, Inc. v. Fed. Ins. Co., No. 900-0288-C (Mass. Dist. Ct. 1992) (no published opinion).
22. Cargill, Inc. v. Nat'l Union Fire Ins. Co., No. A03-187, 2004 WL 51671 (Minn. App. 2004).
23. Nike, Inc. v. Nw. Pac. Indem. Co., 999 P.2d 1197 (Ore. App. 2000).

The insured's employee submitted fraudulent tax returns on behalf of clients to increase the amount of professional fees obtained by the insured accounting firm, and thus higher commissions to himself. The court held that the insured had care, custody, and control of the money it paid the employee and caused such money to be transferred to the employee. When the insured paid the employee his commission, the employee took from the insured money the insured owned and money the employee knew he did not earn. The court concluded that that the commission payments to the employee were an unlawful taking.[24]

An employee of the insured had access to the financial records and accounts of the insured's customer, which she abused by stealing that customer's money for her own use. In its motion to dismiss, the insurer argued that coverage could not apply because the employee had stolen from the customer, not from the insured. On a motion to dismiss, the court held that the definition of theft was not limited to property that belonged to the insured. Instead, the key language was "to the deprivation of the insured." The court found that the employee's taking had ultimately deprived the insured according to the pleadings.[25]

The insured sold petroleum products on credit to a customer. The insured's employee forged letters of credit that supposedly were securing the customer's account. The insured sustained a loss when the customer failed to pay a substantial balance due and it could not recover from the security. The insured's forgery or alteration coverage excluded coverage for any act of an employee except when covered by the "employee theft" insuring agreement. The court affirmed summary judgment for the insurer. Employee theft coverage requires an unlawful taking, and there was no "taking" by the employee. Forgery or alteration coverage and employee theft coverage insure against different risks, even if a forgery committed by an employee that involves an unlawful taking constitutes "employee theft."[26]

---

24. Ryan, LLC v. Nat'l Union Fire Ins. Co., No. 05-22-00286-CV, 2023 WL 2472889 (Tex. App. 2023).
25. Transtar Elec., Inc. v. Charter Oak Fire Ins. Co., No. 3:13CV1837, 2014 WL 252023 (N.D. Ohio 2014).
26. Tesoro Refin. & Mktg. Co. v. Nat'l Union Fire Ins. Co., 833 F.3d 470 (5th Cir. 2016).

3. Is the Loss Direct?

The policy does not contemplate a loss "when a third party is deprived of property and the third party later sues the insured or requires repayment under a contractual provision."[27]

The insured was a marketing company responsible for putting together promotional games and contests for McDonalds. The insured's dishonest employees funneled high-value winning game pieces to specific individuals and received kickbacks from the "winners." The insured argued that the dishonest employee had engaged in theft of the McDonalds pieces that he helped funnel to his accomplices. The court seemed to agree that there had been a theft, but it held that the resulting loss was borne by McDonalds, not the insured, and affirmed the award of summary judgment for the insurer.[28]

Coverage for "theft" was held not to be ambiguous and to cover only direct loss to the insured, not loss to third parties. Furthermore, the third party did not suffer a deprivation by the insured's use of proprietary genetic information because the insured's use of the information did not deprive the third party of its own use of the information.[29]

III.
Forgery/Alteration

While many typical claims involving allegations of forgery or alteration do not involve much in the way of technology (*e.g.* stealing checks from the mail, forged endorsements), technological advances have begun to leave their mark on these claims (*e.g.* e-lending schemes, counterfeit checks).

A. Coverage Issues for Forgery/Alteration Claims

Forgery or alteration coverage provides indemnity for a loss resulting directly from the forgery or alteration of a covered document. Thus, what qualifies as a covered document may prove contentious (e.g., an email

---

27. CP Food & Beverage, Inc. v. United States Fire Ins. Co., 324 F. Supp. 3d 1172 (D. Nev. 2018).
28. Simon Mktg., Inc. v. Gulf Ins. Co., 57 Cal. Rptr. 3d 49 (Cal. App. 2007).
29. Cargill, Inc. v. Nat'l Union Fire Ins. Co., No. A03-187, 2004 WL 51671 (Minn. App. 2004).

containing a fraudulent signature block does not qualify). An issue may also arise where an insured attempts to bundle a group of documents together, one of which qualifies for coverage but does not contain the qualifying defect and another which does not qualify for coverage but does contain the qualifying defect.

Another issue frequently arises within the context of the definition of "forgery," meaning the signing of the name of another person with intent to deceive and excludes the signing of one's own name. Alteration typically is not a defined term leaving courts and parties to employ its ordinary meaning.

Finally, as with employee theft/dishonesty coverage, an issue arises with respect to whether the loss resulted directly from a forgery or alteration. An established body of precedent in the context of fraudulent loan claims finds no direct loss even where a qualifying document bears a qualifying defect where the collateral underlying the transaction is fictitious (*i.e.* fictitious/worthless collateral).

B. Illustrative Cases

1. Is the Document Covered?

The insured sustained a loss as a result of a scheme perpetrated by its workers' compensation adjuster. The adjuster wrote checks against the insured's account, but kept some of them in his office, never sending them to the named payees (which were legitimate entities). His computer program generated ledgers reflecting all of the checks written, irrespective of whether they were negotiated or disbursed. He sent the ledgers to the insured, which would replenish its account based upon the ledgers. The insured did not know that some of the checks reflected in the ledgers had not been sent and would never be negotiated, thereby continuing to replenish its account in excess of the amount the adjuster actually paid out, with the adjuster continuing to convert the excess replenishments. The insured sought recovery of its loss pursuant to the forgery or alteration insuring agreement, and the court affirmed summary judgment for the insurer. The insured's argument that the check ledgers were altered failed because the ledgers were not a covered document.[30]

30. Milwaukee Area Tech. College v. Frontier Adjusters of Milwaukee, 752 N.W.2d 396 (Wis. Ct. App. 2008).

The insured agreed to purchase scrap metal from another entity. It posted a letter of credit for the seller to obtain payment upon shipment of the metal. To draw on the letter of credit, the seller had to present a sight draft and various other documents demonstrating that the metal had been shipped. The letter of credit itself was drawn on a third-party bank. Using fraudulent documents, the seller obtained payment from the letter of credit despite never having shipped the metal. The court reversed summary judgment for the insured, holding that forgery coverage did not cover the loss because none of the fraudulent documents were drawn by or upon the insured or its agent.[31]

Hackers gained access to the insured's computer system and, using employee passwords, were able to gain access to an online banking system and transferred funds from the insured's account. The appellate court affirmed the district court's rejection of the insured's claim that the loss was covered by its forgery or alteration coverage. Electronic transfers were not similar to a check, draft, or other similar negotiable instrument, and there was no signature involved in the effectuation of the transfers.[32]

The insured's payroll director embezzled funds through a scheme that involved him obtaining access to the insured's bank accounts to effect withdrawals that were to be used to pay taxes. The scheme involved him "fraudulently obtaining" the electronic signature of the insured's comptroller on the form giving him authorization to access the bank accounts (but the decision does not explain how the signature was "fraudulently obtained"). The insured sought coverage for its loss from, inter alia, its forgery or alteration coverage. The court denied the insurer's motion to dismiss this aspect of the claim, holding that the insured stated a claim because, while the authorization form containing the "fraudulently obtained" electronic signature alone was not a document covered by the forgery or alteration insuring agreement, the authorization form and the ACH withdrawals that resulted could be construed together to constitute a covered document.[33]

The insured believed that it had entered into an agreement with a Costa Rican entity to purchase scrap metal. It posted a letter of credit for the seller to obtain payment upon shipment of the metal. To draw on the letter of credit, the seller had to present a sight draft and various other documents

31. Parkans Int'l LLC v. Zurich Ins. Co., 299 F.3d 514 (5th Cir. 2002).
32. Metro Brokers, Inc. v. Transp. Ins. Co., 603 F. App'x 833 (11th 2015).
33. Success Healthcare, LLC v. Zurich Am. Ins. Co., No.14-81423, 2015 WL 11439019 (S.D. Fla. 2015).

demonstrating that the metal had been shipped, such as an invoice, packing slip, and bill of lading. The purported seller presented the sight draft and the other documents and received payment from the letter of credit. All but the sight draft were forgeries, and the insured never received the shipment of metal. The court granted the insured summary judgment, holding that the loss was covered by the insured's forgery or alteration coverage. Despite stating that it was obligated to apply the "plain and ordinary meaning" of the policy's terms, the court considered the sight draft (which was not forged) and the other documents (none of which constitute a covered document) together and concluded that, taken together, they constituted a covered instrument. The court also determined that the requirement that the covered instrument be "drawn upon you" is ambiguous and construed the supposed ambiguity against the insurer.[34]

The insured sustained a loss when an imposter sent e-mails that purported to be from the insured's majority owner to the insured's controller, directing her to transfer funds to the imposter's bank account. Investigation revealed that the deceptive e-mails were not the result of any hacking or unauthorized access to the insured's computer systems. The court rejected the insured's claim against the forgery or alteration insuring agreement, holding that, while the e-mails were a direction to pay money, they were not similar to checks, drafts, or promissory notes.[35]

Hackers infiltrated the insured's e-mail system and sent an e-mail to an employee about a supposed confidential acquisition, which purported to be from the insured's president. Because the e-mail system was based upon Gmail, the e-mail had an added apparent layer of authenticity because Gmail automatically populated the e-mail with a picture of the president. The hacker subsequently called the employee and directed her to arrange a wire of a substantial sum in connection with this supposed transaction. The employee explained that others needed to approve the wire, and the hacker sent another e-mail to the employees about the wire, which again populated with the president's picture. The employees approved the wire, the proceeds of which were lost. The court upheld the insurer's rejection of the aspect of the insured's claim that sought recovery pursuant to forgery or alteration coverage. The coverage applied to forgery

---

34. Omnisource Corp. v. CNA/Transcont'l Ins. Co., 949 F. Supp. 681 (N.D. Ind. 1996).
35. Sanderina, LLC v. Great Am. Ins. Co., No. 18-cv-00772, 2019 WL 4307854 (D. Nev. 2019).

or alteration of a "financial instrument," and the fraudulent e-mails were not a "financial instrument."[36]

Hackers accessed the insured's e-mail system and sent phony wire transfer instructions to the insured's bank, directing the transfer of substantial sums to the hackers' account. The hackers cut and pasted signatures of the insured's officers on to wire transfer forms submitted to the bank. The court rejected the insured's claim that the loss was covered by its forgery or alteration coverage, concluding that the wire transfer forms were not the type of document covered by the insuring agreement, which protects against forgery or alteration of negotiable instruments and similar documents. A factor in the court's decision was that the insured declined to purchase the funds transfer fraud coverage offered by the insurer, which would have covered this loss. The policy was clear that the coverages do not overlap.[37]

The insured's employee received an e-mail purporting to be from the insured's president asking her to wire a substantial sum to another account. The e-mail was from a hacker and the wired money was lost. The court rejected the insured's claim that the forgery or alteration insuring agreement covered its loss. The fraudulent e-mail directing the employee to effect the wire transfer was not similar to a negotiable instrument and thus was not the type of document to which the coverage applied.[38]

The insured, a payroll services provider, sustained a loss through a sophisticated scheme carried out by an imposter. The insured sought to recover its loss pursuant to the forgery or alteration insuring agreement, contending that e-mails sent by the imposter directing the transfer of electronic funds constituted "checks, drafts, promissory notes, or similar written promises, orders, or directions to pay." The appellate court affirmed the lower court's award of summary judgment for the insurer, holding that e-mails do not fit within the category of covered instruments.[39]

The insured worked with an independent broker to purchase specialty cars and sell them to buyers. The broker would send a title application,

36. Medidata Sols., Inc. v. Fed. Ins. Co., 268 F. Supp. 3d 471 (S.D.N.Y. 2017), aff'd, 729 F. App'x 117 (2d Cir. 2018)
37. Ryeco, LLC v. Selective Ins. Co., 539 F. Supp. 3d 399 (E.D. Pa. 2021).
38. Midlothian Enters., Inc. v. Owners Ins. Co., 439 F. Supp. 3d 737 (E.D. Va. 2020).
39. Michael A. Veneman, CPA PSC v. Travelers Cas. Ins. Co., No. 2022-CA-0021-MR, 2023 WL 3261555 (Ky. Ct. App. 2023).

purchase order, warranty disclaimer, odometer disclosure statement, and lease agreement to the insured, which then would issue a check to the broker to purchase the cars. The transactions were fraudulent; the documents supplied by the broker were forged and the insured never received the cars. The court affirmed summary judgment for the insurer dismissing the claim against the policy's forgery coverage on the ground that none of the forged documents were a covered instrument.[40]

An imposter pretending to be the president of the insured sent e-mails to the insured's employee and the insured's bank to arrange to have the employee authorized to effect wire transfers. The e-mails included the president's usual "signature block" (which did not include a signature) and company logo. The imposter then, by e-mail, directed the employee to make two wire transfers. She arranged for the bank to make the first but not the second, eventually determining that the e-mails were not legitimate. The appellate court affirmed a jury verdict that the loss resulted directly from forgery of a covered instrument. The court held that the "similar written promises, orders or directions to pay a sum certain in money" clause was "broad enough" to include the imposter's e-mails, as "negotiable" does not appear in the clause—a conclusion that is inconsistent with the principle of ejusdem generis.[41]

The insured sustained a loss when it paid its vendor for pallets that the vendor did not actually deliver. The payments were based upon the vendor's submission of a package of documents reflecting supposed deliveries, which included delivery tickets bearing the forged signature of a representative of the insured. The court affirmed summary judgment for the insurer, holding that delivery tickets were simply evidence of delivery and were not written promises, orders, or directions to pay money.[42]

2. Is There a "Forgery" or Alteration?

The insured, a premium financing business, received fraudulent applications from the Charles McMahon Insurance Agency, which was owned by Charles McMahon, Sr. Charles McMahon, Jr., worked for the

40. Frank Shoop, Inc. v. TIG Ins. Co., No. 2007-CA-000691-MR, 2009 WL 874535 (Ky. Ct. App. 2009).
41. Cent. Mut. Ins. Co. v. Reliance Prop. Mgmt., Inc., No. 05-21-00071-CV, 2022 WL 1657031 (Tex. App. 2022).
42. Leicht Transfer & Storage Co. v. Pallet Cent. Enters., Inc., 928 N.W.2d 534 (Wis. 2019).

agency and submitted the fraudulent applications. McMahon Jr. converted the checks issued by the insured, which were made payable to the agency, by endorsing them in the name of the agency and depositing them into his personal account. McMahon Jr. had general authority to endorse checks on the agency's behalf. The court affirmed judgment for the insured, rejecting the insurer's argument that there was no forgery because McMahon Jr.'s endorsement of the checks included part of his own name, calling the argument "absurd." The court also said that the endorsements constituted forgeries because McMahon Jr. signed the name of another with intent to deceive, even if he had general authority to endorse checks on the agency's behalf.[43]

The insured law firm was solicited by e-mail by a supposed potential client located overseas to represent the potential client in a dispute, and it agreed to do so. The law firm then was advised that the dispute had been settled and that the other party would send the settlement payment. The law firm received what appeared to be a certified check issued by large bank. The client told the law firm to deposit the check, keep a portion of the proceeds for its fees, and send the rest to the client. The law firm did so. The certified check proved to be fraudulent and the amount the law firm paid to the supposed client was lost. The court held that forgery coverage applied. Although the insured could not prove who signed the fake certified check, the court assumed that the fraudster would not have signed his or her own name to the check. The court also rejected the insurer's curious argument that the loss was not covered because the "check" was a counterfeit, and that coverage applied only to forged checks drawn on the bank's actual certified check stock. The insuring agreement, curiously, did not appear to require that the forged check be drawn by or upon the insured or by one acting as the insured's agent.[44]

The insured sustained a loss resulting from a fraudulent e-mail scheme. Its employee received e-mails that appeared to be from the insured's president, directing that the employee make various electronic payments to a vendor. The e-mails were from an imposter and the money transferred was lost. The insured sought recovery of its loss from its commercial crime policy, which provided coverage for loss resulting directly from forgery or alteration of, inter alia, "orders or directions to pay a sum certain in money that you or your agent has issued, or that was

43. Great Am. Ins. Co. v. AFS/IBEX Fin. Servs., Inc., 612 F.3d 800 (5th Cir. 2010).

44. Morris James LLP v. Cont'l Cas. Co., 928 F. Supp. 2d 816 (D. Del. 2013).

issued by someone who impersonates you or your agent." The court held that this provision provided coverage, as the e-mails constituted "directions to pay a sum certain in money" that were issued by someone impersonating the insured. The court appeared to ignore the policy's requirement that the "orders or directions" have been forged or altered.[45]

The insureds sustained a loss when someone hacked into their bank accounts and stole funds. They asserted a claim against their commercial crime policy on a number of grounds, including that the loss was covered by the policy's forgery or alteration coverage. The court summarily rejected the claim. There was no forgery, as the hacker did not sign anything.[46]

The insured's bookkeeper embezzled substantial sums from the insured through a scheme that included her making checks out to herself or her husband and burying them in a pile of checks for the insured's authorized signatory to sign, which he did. In affirming judgment for the insured, the court rejected the insurer's argument that there was no forgery. The policy did not define "forgery." The court looked to the definition under criminal law, of a document "falsely made, completed, or altered" and concluded, puzzlingly, that the bookkeeper was "essentially altering checks" prior to the insured signing them.[47]

The insured sustained a loss as a result of a scheme perpetrated by its workers' compensation adjuster. The adjuster wrote checks against the insured's account, but kept some of them in his office, never sending them to the named payees (which were legitimate entities). The insured sought recovery of its loss pursuant to the forgery or alteration insuring agreement, and the court affirmed summary judgment for the insurer. There was no forgery of the checks, as the adjuster signed his own name and made them payable to legitimate entities.[48]

The insured sustained a loss when its payroll company withdrew more money from its accounts than the payroll company was paying in payroll

---

45. Ad Advertising Design, Inc. v. Sentinel Ins. Co., 344 F. Supp. 3d 1175 (D. Mont. 2018).
46. Metal Pro Roofing, LLC v. Cincinnati Ins. Co., 130 N.E.3d 653 (Ind. Ct. App. 2019).
47. Piles Chevrolet Pontiac Buick, Inc. v. Auto Owners Ins. Co., Nos. 2011-CA-002317-MR, 2011-CA-002340-MR, 2013 WL 2120319 (Ky. Ct. App. 2013).
48. Milwaukee Area Tech. College v. Frontier Adjusters of Milwaukee, 752 N.W.2d 396 (Wis. Ct. App. 2008).

taxes on the insured's behalf and kept the excess. The payroll company disguised the fraud by providing an IRS tax form to the insured reflecting the amount withdrawn from the accounts and a different tax form to the IRS in the reduced amount that the payroll company was remitting in taxes. The decision does not state whether either of the tax forms were altered from an accurate original. The court denied the insurer's summary judgment motion, accepting the insured's argument that the payroll company's remittance of less to the IRS than its computer program calculated should be withdrawn from the insured's account for payroll taxes could constitute an "alteration" of "instruments."[49]

The insureds sustained a loss when someone hacked into their bank accounts and stole funds. They asserted a claim against their commercial crime policy on a number of grounds, including that the loss was covered by the policy's forgery or alteration insuring agreement. The court summarily rejected the claim. There was no alteration, as the insureds failed to identify any document that the hacker changed.[50]

3. *Is the Loss Direct?*

The insured submitted a claim seeking to recover under both the forgery or alteration insuring agreement and the securities insuring agreement for a loss after it extended credit secured by non-existent collateral. The court found the insured could not recover because the loss resulted from worthless collateral, not forgery.[51]

The insured submitted a claim arising out of a loss on a warehouse line of credit. The underlying mortgages were fictitious. The court held that the insured could not recover under the forgery insuring agreement because the underlying loans did not occur and the bank would have been unable to enforce the loans even if legitimately executed.[52]

The insured sought to recover losses sustained after the bank approved a loan secured by forged stock certificates. The court denied the insured

---

49. Orgill/Singer & Assocs., Inc. v. Fed. Ins. Co., 943 F. Supp. 2d 1141 (D. Nev. 2013).
50. Metal Pro Roofing, LLC v. Cincinnati Ins. Co., 130 N.E.3d 653 (Ind. Ct. App. 2019).
51. Forcht Bank, N.A. v. BancInsure, Inc., 514 F. App'x 586, 591 (6th Cir. 2013).
52. Flagstar Bank, FSB v. Fed. Ins. Co., 260 F. App'x 820, 821-22 (6th Cir. 2007).

the requested relief, finding that, because the stock certificates were worthless, the bank would have suffered the same loss regardless of the alleged forgery.[53]

IV.
Computer Fraud

A. Coverage Issues for Computer Fraud Claims

Because computers have become necessary and commonplace, we frequently see losses involving computers. Insureds often seek coverage under computer fraud insuring agreements, without analyzing the substance of the actual coverage. The narrow coverage afforded for computer fraud is intended to cover unauthorized access as a result of a system breach and transmission of property without any intervention or awareness of the insured's employees. Thus, to implicate coverage, the perpetrator must forcibly and without authorization access the insured's computer system.

In a typical claim, a perpetrator hacks into the computer network of an insured company, gains access to the company's bank account or payment system, and facilitates transfers without the insured's knowledge and without any action taken by the insured's employees. However, insureds have attempted to seek coverage under computer fraud for ransomware and social engineering attacks. Computer fraud is intended to cover neither. As a result, many insurers limit coverage through exclusions or sublimited coverage endorsements.

B. Illustrative Cases

1. Claims Under Computer Fraud Insuring Agreements

The insured retained a vendor to handle preparation of the insured's payroll, payment of payroll taxes, and delivery of payroll checks. In order to allow the vendor to perform agreed upon payroll and payroll tax services, the insured executed an ACH authorization, which authorized the insured to obtain payment of the insured's approved invoices by initiating ACH transfers of funds from the insured's bank account to the vendor's

53. Bank of Bozeman v. BancInsure, Inc., 404 F. App'x 117, 119 (9th Cir. 2010).

bank account. The vendor provided invoices to the insured and once the insured approved the invoices, the vendor initiated an ACH transfer to move sufficient funds from the insured's bank account to the vendor's bank account. The vendor failed to remit the insured's taxes. The court determined that the insured authorized the transfers and thus, the transfers were not fraudulent caused. Accordingly, the court held that no coverage existed under the computer fraud insuring agreement.[54]

The insured operated a network allowing consumers to put money into general-purpose reloadable debit cards issued by banks. The insured sold the "chits" to the consumer and the consumer called the insured to redeem the chit and have the value transferred to the card. Fraudsters manipulated a glitch in the computerized interactive-telephone system that allowed them to redeem chits multiple times. The court held that the fraudsters' use of telephones to interface with the insured's computer system was sufficient to satisfy the "use of a computer" requirement in the policy.[55]

Fraudsters utilized fraudulent purchase orders, post-dated checks, and a purported bank guaranty of checks transmitted via facsimile to defraud the insured. The insured received these documents from the fraudster and the insured purchased phone cards, providing them to the fraudster. The court held that the faxed post-dated checks and bank guaranties did not fraudulently cause a transfer and thus, no coverage existed under the computer fraud insuring agreement.[56]

The insured's employee placed false and fraudulent entries on the insured's records to benefit one of the insured's customers. The customer signed an agreement allowing the insured to process debits and credits to the customer's account through ACH transfers. The employee manipulated the insured's system to create fraudulent credits to the customer such that the system did not transfer funds owed from the customer to the insured. The court held that coverage existed for transfers the employee made from the insured's account, but not for any items that the insured delivered to the customer.[57]

---

54. Pestmaster Servs., Inc. v. Travelers Cas. and Sur. Co., 656 F. App'x 332, 333 (9th Cir. 2016).
55. Interactive Commc'n. Int'l, Inc. v. Great Am. Ins. Co., 731 F. App'x 929, 933 (11th Cir. 2018).
56. Brightpoint, Inc. v. Zurich Am. Ins. Co., No. 1:04-CV-2085-SEB-JPG, 2006 WL 693377, at *7 (S.D. Ind. 2006).
57. Lykins Oil Co. v. Travelers Cas. and Sur. Co., Case No. 1:08-cv-546, 2009 WL 10679056, at *8-9 (S.D. Ohio 2009).

The insured provided premium financing in the insurance industry and entered into an agreement with a third party. The agreement contemplated that the third party would create and sign premium finance applications on behalf of the clients. The insured then sent a check to the insurance company for the purchase price of the insurance, and the clients would send regular payments to the insured. The third party's son submitted false applications to dupe the insured into issuing checks to his company and kept the funds. The court held that no coverage existed under the computer fraud insuring agreement and noted that "the language of these provisions indicate that they are designed to cover losses directly stemming from fraud perpetrated by use of a computer."[58]

The insured provided ACH transactions and related payroll services. The insured had a written agreement with a remarketer in which the insured offered its ACH services to route payments from the remarketer's clients to those clients' employees. An employee of the remarketer manipulated "batch files" such that the insured paid out funds that it never received. The court held that there was no fraudulent entry into the insured's computer system because the persons uploading the batch files were authorized to conduct business with the insured.[59]

This case involves the submission of fraudulent Medicare claims in a computerized billing system that allowed payment for claims for unprovided services paid through the insured's computer system. This case was decided under a computer systems fraud insuring agreement with similar, relevant language to the computer fraud insuring agreement. The court held that the insured's loss was not covered because the insuring agreement applies to losses resulting directly from fraudulent access, not to losses from the content submitted by authorized users.[60]

2. Social Engineering Schemes For Which the Insured Sought Coverage Under a Computer Fraud Insuring Agreement

Social engineering scheme for which the insured sought coverage under a computer fraud insuring agreement: A fraudster instructed the

58. Great Am. Ins. Co. v. AFS/IBEX Fin. Servs., Inc., Civil Action No. 3:07-CV-924-O, 2008 WL 2795205, at *14 (N.D. Tex. 2008).
59. Cachet Fin. Servs. v. Berkley Ins. Co., Case No. 2:22-cv-01157-SPG-JEM, 2023 WL 2558413, at *7-8 (C.D. Cal. 2023).
60. Universal Am. Corp. v. Nat. Union Fire Ins. Co., 25 N.Y.3d 675, 682-83 (N.Y. Ct. App. 2015).

insured by telephone to change the bank-account information for payments to a vendor. The insured required the fraudster provide the change of account instruction by formal request on the vendor's letterhead, which the fraudster did by electronic mail. The insured called the telephone number on the letterhead sent by the fraudster and approved the bank-account change. The insured then paid out approximately $7 million for legitimate vendor invoices to the fraudster. The court, applying Texas law, held that there was not a covered loss because the loss did not result directly from the use of any computer to fraudulently cause a transfer.[61]

A fraudster impersonating the insured's vendor sent emails to the insured's employee asking the employee to change the vendor's wire information. The employee changed the wire information and the insured sent funds to the fraudster's account. The court rejected the insurer's attempt to limit the definition of computer fraud to hacking and similar behaviors and held that the fraudster's actions constituted computer fraud under the policy.[62]

A fraudster sent an email to the insured's account payable clerk purporting to be her superior requesting the account payable clerk make wire transfers to a vendor's bank account. The accounts payable clerk made the payments to the vendor. The court distinguished other precedent to find that initiating a wire transfer did not constitute the authorization of payment. Thus, the court held that coverage existed under the computer fraud insuring agreement.[63]

A fraudster sent an email to the insured's accounts payable assistant purporting to be one of the insured's vendors. The fraudster requested the insured change the vendor's method of receiving payments to electronic ACH transfers. After numerous emails and some time passed, the insured changed the vendor's method of payment and sent numerous ACH payments to the fraudster. The court held that the fraudster's actions constituted computer fraud, reasoning that the phrase "use of a computer"

---

61. Apache Corp. v. Great Am. Ins. Co., 662 F. App'x 252, 258 (5th Cir. 2016).
62. Am. Tolling Ctr., Inc. v. Travelers Cas. and Sur. Co., 895 F.3d 455, 461-62 (6th Cir. 2018).
63. Ernst & Haas Mgmt. Co., Inc. v. Hiscox, 23 F.4th 1195, 1200-01 (9th Cir. 2022) (*distinguishing* Pestmaster Services, Inc. v. Travelers Casualty and Surety Co., No. CV 13-5039-JFW, 2014 WL 3844627 (C.D. Cal. July 17, 2014)).

encompasses a broad range of activities including sending emails, and is not limited to computer hacking.[64]

The insured received an email from a fraudster purporting to be a North Carolina attorney assisting the attorney's China-based client in collecting a debt. The fraudster also sent an email to the insured purporting to be the director of the China-based client and what appeared to be an "Official Check" made payable to the insured. The fraudster then sent the insured instructions via email to wire funds in the amount of the Official Check from the insured's trust account to the fraudster's account. The court held that the fraudster's email exchanges with the insured constituted computer fraud.[65]

In a "spoofing" case for which the insured sought coverage under a computer fraud insuring agreement, fraudsters used a spoofing code to allow the fraudsters to send messages appearing to come from a high-ranking member of the insured's organization. The court held that the fraudsters' actions were a fraudulent entry of data into the computer system and made change to a data element. Thus, the insured's losses were covered by the policy.[66]

A fraudster sent emails to the insured's employee purporting to be from the insured's client. The insured then wired money to the fraudster. The court determined that the fraudster's emails did not constitute an unauthorized entry into the insured's computer system.[67]Social engineering scheme for which the insured sought coverage under a computer and funds transfer insuring clause: The insured's executives received an email from a fraudster purporting to be from a law firm paralegal asking the insured's chief executive officer to transfer money to a bank account in Hong Kong. The court held that the fraudulent emails did not implicate a "computer and funds transfer" insuring clause.[68]

---

64. City of Unalaska v. Nat'l Union Fire Ins. Co., 591 F.Supp.3d 440, 451 (D. Alaska 2022).
65. Owens, Schine & Nicola, P.C. v. Travelers Cas. & Sur. Co., No. CV095024601, 2010 WL 4226958, at *4, *vacated*, 2012 WL 12246940 (Conn. Super. Ct. 2010).
66. Medidata Sol., Inc. v. Fed. Ins. Co., 729 F. App'x 117, 118 (2d Cir. 2018).
67. Taylor & Lieberman v. Fed. Ins. Co., 681 F. App'x 627, 629 (9th Cir. 2017).
68. Children's Apparel Network Ltd. v. Twin City Fire Ins. Co., 18 Civ. 10322, 2019 WL 3162199, at *5 (S.D.N.Y. 2019).

A fraudster, purporting to be the insured's vendor, sent emails to the insured requesting that the insured change the payment information for the vendor. The insured sent the vendor's payment to the insured. The court held that the receipt of an email is not an "unauthorized access or entry into Plaintiff's system." The court also noted that "the Court is convinced that to trigger coverage under the Policy, it requires more than just the use of fraudulent information."[69]

V.
Funds Transfer Fraud

A. Coverage Issues for Funds Transfer Fraud Claims

Similar to Computer Fraud, the central issue that arises under Funds Transfer Fraud is whether the circumstances of the claim trigger the narrow coverage. While computer fraud coverage is designed to cover unauthorized access to/use of the insured's computer system to cause a transfer, funds transfer fraud coverage is designed to cover situations where a fraudster induces a financial institution to allow funds to be withdrawn from the insured's account by posing as the insured and submitting a fraudulent instruction. However, neither provides coverage for circumstances in which the insured is induced to process a transfer requested by the threat actor. In that way, Funds Transfer Fraud also requires the insured and its employees have no knowledge of or involvement in the threat actor's conduct; instead, the threat actor impersonates the insured and dupes the insured's bank into sending money.

What constitutes a fraudulent instruction differs amongst policies. Typically, the fraudulent instruction must have been purportedly issued by the insured without the insured's knowledge or consent and the instruction must have been sent directly to a financial institution (the insured's bank) – not to the insured for its employees to route to the financial institution.

---

69. Kraft Chem. Co. v. Fed. Ins. Co., No. 13 M2 002568, 2016 WL 4938493, at *6 (Ill. Cir. Ct. 2016).

B. Illustrative Cases

1. Claims Under Funds Transfer Fraud Insuring Agreements

The insured retained a vendor to handle preparation of the insured's payroll, payment of payroll taxes, and delivery of payroll checks. In order to allow the vendor to perform agreed upon payroll and payroll tax services, the insured executed an ACH authorization, which authorized the insured to obtain payment of the insured's approved invoices by initiating ACH transfers of funds from the insured's bank account to the vendor's bank account. The vendor would provide invoices to the insured and once the insured approved the invoices, the vendor would initiate an ACH transfer to move sufficient funds from the insured's bank account to the vendor's bank account. The vendor failed to remit the insured's taxes. The court determined that no coverage existed under the funds transfer fraud insuring agreement because the transfers were expressly authorized.[70]

The insured provided ACH transactions and related payroll services. The insured had a written agreement with a remarketer in which the insured offered its ACH services to route payments from the remarketer's clients to those clients' employees. An employee of the remarketer manipulated "batch files" such that the insured paid out funds that it never received. The court held that the insured failed to demonstrate that the batch files were "altered" under the plain meaning of the term.[71]

The insured's employee placed false and fraudulent entries on the insured's records to benefit one of the insured's customers. The customer signed an agreement allowing the insured to process debits and credits to the customer's account through ACH transfers. The employee manipulated the insured's system to create fraudulent credits to the customer such that the system did not transfer funds owed from the customer to the insured. The court held that no coverage existed under the funds transfer fraud insuring agreement because its loss did not constitute a transfer. But, the court did find that the use of the word "you" in the

---

70. Pestmaster Servs., Inc. v. Travelers Cas. and Sur. Co., 656 F. App'x 332, 333 (9th Cir. 2016).
71. Cachet Fin. Servs. v. Berkley Ins. Co., Case No. 2:22-cv-01157-SPG-JEM, 2023 WL 2558413, at *8 (C.D. Cal. 2023).

insuring agreement was ambiguous under Ohio law and does not necessarily include all of the insured's employees.[72]

The insured provided premium financing in the insurance industry and entered into an agreement with a third party. The agreement contemplated that the third party would create and sign premium finance applications on behalf of the clients. The insured then sent a check to the insurance company for the purchase price of the insurance, and the clients sent regular payments to the insured. The third party's son submitted false applications to dupe the insured into issuing checks to his company and kept the funds. The court held that no coverage existed under the funds transfer fraud insuring agreement because the insured's losses were caused by a forgery, which was expressly excluded from the definition of instructions in the funds transfer fraud insuring agreement.[73]

2. Social Engineering Schemes For Which the Insured Sought Coverage Under a Funds Transfer Fraud Insuring Agreement

A fraudster, purporting to be a lender's employee, sent the insured's employee fraudulent writing instructions. The insured wired funds to the fraudster. The court held that the insured's loss was covered under the funds transfer fraud insuring agreement.[74]

A fraudster sent an email to the insured's account payable clerk purporting to be her superior requesting the account payable clerk make wire transfers to a vendor's bank account. The policy defined fraudulent instruction to include "an electronic . . . instruction initially received by You which purports to have been transmitted by an Employee but which was in fact fraudulently transmitted by someone else without Your or the Employee's knowledge or consent." The court held that the fraudster's email constituted a fraudulent instruction as defined by the policy.[75]

---

72. Lykins Oil Co. v. Travelers Cas. and Sur. Co., Case No. 1:08-cv-546, 2009 WL 10679056, at *10 (S.D. Ohio 2009).

73. Great Am. Ins. Co. v. AFS/IBEX Fin. Servs., Inc., Civil Action No. 3:07-CV-924-O, 2008 WL 2795205, at *15 (N.D. Tex. 2008), *aff'd on other grounds*, 612 F.3d 800.

74. Valero Title Inc. v. RLI Ins. Co., No. 22-20155, 2023 WL 1434270, at *3 (5th Cir. 2023).

75. Ernst & Haas Mgmt. Co., Inc. v. Hiscox, 23 F.4th 1195, 1203 (9th Cir. 2022).

A fraudster sent emails to the insured's employee purporting to be from the insured's client. The insured then wired money to the fraudster. The court held that no coverage existed under the funds transfer fraud insuring agreement because the insured knew about the wire transfers and the instructions were sent to the insured, not a financial institution.[76]

A fraudster purported to be the insured's managing director and directed the insured's controller to wire funds to an attorney who would provide further information. The insured's controller obtained the wire information from the fraudster purporting to be the attorney and after a number of communications with the fraudster and the bank, wired money to the fraudster's bank account. The court, applying Georgia law, held that the fraudster's emails purporting to be the managing director and the attorney together met the definition of fraudulent instruction under the policy.[77]

The fraudster sent an email purporting to be the insured's vendor advising that future payments to the vendor should be routed to a new bank account. The insured made payments to the fraudster's new bank account. The policy at issue provided coverage for loss resulting directly from funds transfer fraud that causes the transfer, payment, or delivery of covered property from the premises or transfer account to a person, place, or account beyond the insured's control, without the insured's knowledge or consent. The court held that the insured did not suffer a covered loss because three of the insured's employees authorized the transfer and thus, the transfer could not have been without the insured's knowledge.[78]

The insured's executives received an email from a fraudster purporting to be from a law firm paralegal asking the insured's chief executive officer to transfer money to a bank account in Hong Kong. The court held that the fraudulent emails did not implicate a "computer and funds transfer" insuring clause because the instruction was sent to the insured, not directly to the insured's bank.[79]

---

76. Taylor & Lieberman v. Fed. Ins. Co., 681 F. App'x 627, 629 (9th Cir. 2016).
77. Principle Sol. Grp., LLC v. Ironshore Indem., Inc., 944 F.3d 886, 891 (11th Cir. 2019).
78. Miss. Silicon Holdings, LLC v. AXIS Ins. Co., 440 F. Supp. 3d 575, 585 (N.D. Miss. 2020), *aff'd on similar ground*, 843 F. App'x 581.
79. Children's Apparel Network Ltd. v. Twin City Fire Ins. Co., 18 Civ. 10322, 2019 WL 3162199, at *5 (S.D.N.Y. 2019).

Fraudsters used a spoofing code to allow the fraudsters to send messages appearing to come from a high-ranking member of the insured's organization. The court stated that the "fact that the accounts payable employee willingly pressed the send button on the bank transfer does not transform the bank wire into a valid transaction[,]" and found coverage under a funds transfer fraud insuring agreement.[80]

The insured was tricked via email into transferring funds to fraudsters. The court held that no coverage existed because the fraudster did not send instructions to the insured's bank and the instructions were not issued, forged, or altered without the insured's consent.[81]

VI.
Social Engineering Fraud

A. Coverage Issues for Social Engineering Fraud Claims

With the evolution of technology, perpetrators no longer even need to breach an insured's computer system to steal an insured's funds—instead, perpetrators pose as an insured's legitimate vendor, client, or employee to trick the insured into sending money to a fraudulent account. The perpetrator typically uses a computer to try to bait an employee of the insured company to voluntarily send money to the perpetrator. The target is typically an employee in the accounting department or someone with authority to make or initiate payments to third parties (i.e., vendors/clients). To accomplish the scheme, the perpetrator may breach the insured's system or a vendor's/client's system to send an email from the actual email account or spoof an email account by creating a fictitious/dummy email account similar to the legitimate email address. The success of social engineering schemes depends on human error.

Most insurers offer social engineering fraud as an additional coverage subject to a separate deductible and sublimit. Because insureds' losses are typically in excess of the sublimit, they may seek coverage under computer fraud (arguing the perpetrator used a computer) or funds transfer fraud (arguing the financial institution received a direction to transfer funds) to obtain the benefit of the higher limits. Generally, the precedent is split over

---

80. Medidata Sol., Inc. v. Fed. Ins. Co., 268 F.Supp.3d 471, 480, *aff'd on other grounds*, 729 F. App'x 117 (S.D.N.Y. 2019).

81. Sanderina, LLC v. Great Am. Ins. Co., Case No.: 2:18-cv-00772-JAD-DJA, 2019 WL 4307854, at *3 (D. Nev. 2019).

whether there is coverage under computer fraud and funds transfer fraud. In response, many insurers implement funneling exclusions to expressly limit coverage of social engineering fraud so that an insured cannot also obtain coverage under computer or funds transfer fraud insuring agreements.

Social engineering coverage does not cover impersonation of just anyone—it only covers impersonation of an employee of the insured, a vendor, or a client of the insured. Because the coverage depends on a third party impersonating an employee, vendor, or client, those terms are specifically defined. With respect to a vendor or client, most forms require a pre-existing relationship between the insured and the impersonated individual or entity as an additional level of risk mitigation, given the prevalence of and relative ease in attempting social engineering schemes.

B. Illustrative Cases

A fraudster emailed fraudulent invoices to the insured's purchasing manager purporting to be from one of the insured's vendors. The fraudulent invoices instructed the insured to pay the invoices through wire transfer to a bank account number that was different from the bank account to which the insured had previously paid the vendor. After emailing the fraudulent invoices to the insured's purchasing manager, the insured hacked into the purchasing manager's email and, impersonating the purchasing manager, forwarded the invoices to the insured's CEO. The insured's CEO called the vendor to confirm the bank account change but was unable to reach the vendor and left a voicemail. Prior to receiving any response from the vendor, the insured initiated two wire transfers to the fraudster's bank account. The court held that the entity (referred to as a vendor in this summary) was a vendor as the entity clearly had a genuine, pre-existing arrangement with the insured. The court also held that the insured's purchasing manager was clearly an employee and the fraudster impersonated the purchasing manager. The court continued to find that the insured's loss clearly met the definition of social-engineering fraud.[82]

The insured was hired as a settlement agent to close a residential real estate transaction. The insured's representative received an email from a fraudster purporting to be a representative of the seller's lienholder providing instructions for how to transfer the payoff funds. The insured

82. SJ Comp., LLC v. Travelers Cas. and Sur. Co., 621 F. Supp. 3d 962, 971-72 (D. Minn. 2022).

followed the fraudster's instructions and wired money to the fraudster. The court determined that the representative of the seller's lienholder was not an employee, customer, client, or vendor of the insured. Thus, the court held that no coverage existed under a social engineering fraud insuring agreement.[83]

This case involves a social engineering scheme for which the insured sought coverage under a computer and funds transfer insuring clause. The insured's executives received an email from a fraudster purporting to be from a law firm paralegal asking the insured's chief executive officer to transfer money to a bank account in Hong Kong. The court held that the insured's president constituted an employee and an owner of the company, and that a paralegal at insured's law firm was a vendor. Thus, the court determined that the insured's loss was from deception fraud.[84]

VII. Conclusion

The advent of evolving technologies used by employees and third parties alike to execute theft schemes and other crimes forced novel interpretations by some courts in the context of standard language in fidelity and crime insurance forms. While employee theft/dishonesty and forgery/alteration coverage held closely to established precedent, the electronic-based coverages (*i.e.* computer fraud, funds transfer fraud, and social engineering fraud) have seen some outlier decisions. However, as forms change to address circumstances where courts have misinterpreted the coverage afforded, the distinct differences between the various insuring agreements and the risks assumed have reemerged.

In the technology context, analyzing the particular policy language at issue is paramount, as is analyzing and understanding the true activity conducted under the mask of technology.

---

83. Star Title Partners of Palm Harbor v. Ill. Union Ins. Co., No. 21-13343, 2022 WL 4075048, at *4 (11th Cir. 2022).

84. Children's Apparel Network Ltd. v. Twin City Fire Ins. Co., 18 Civ. 10322, 2019 WL 3162199, at *4 (S.D.N.Y. 2019).

CHAPTER 10

TECHNOLOGY-BASED INQUIRIES, REQUESTS, AND DISCOVERY—HOW TO GET THE COMPUTER SYSTEM AND FORENSIC INFORMATION YOU NEED

Katherine Musbach

I.
Introduction

With any claimed cyber-related loss, whether submitted under the Financial Institution Bond or a crime policy, understanding exactly what did or did not happen within the computer system, along with the requisite source documentation evidencing as much, is essential. Whether you are adjusting a claim or involved in the initial stages of discovery in litigation, it is important to understand the key policy provisions and key information needed to evaluate coverage. This chapter will outline: (1) the applicable policy language and distinctions among computer fraud, funds transfer fraud, social engineering fraud, and computer restoration coverage; and (2) the information you may want to request to evaluate coverage for the particular claim.

II.
Coverages to Review for Cyber-Based Claims

While every claim is unique, cyber-based claims should generally be reviewed by consulting the computer fraud insuring agreement, restoration coverage, the funds transfer fraud insuring agreement, and social engineering coverage (which is typically added via endorsement). Depending on the form and whether the insured has a crime policy or bond, computer fraud coverage may also be added via endorsement. You will have to determine whether, based on the facts of the claim, you should review other coverages as well. Each of these coverages have general requirements and exclusions that should be evaluated in reaching a claim determination.

A. Computer Fraud and Restoration Coverage

There are several different computer fraud insuring agreements and a few exclusions that are typically implicated by these claims. In one of the seminal computer fraud cases, *Universal Am. Corp.*,[1] the New York Court of Appeals considered the following language, which is close to the language you may find in an Insurance Services Office, Inc. ("ISO") form:

> COMPUTER SYSTEMS FRAUD
> Loss resulting directly from a fraudulent
> (1) entry of Electronic Data or Computer Program into, or
> (2) change of Electronic Data or Computer Program within the Insured's proprietary Computer System . . . provided that the entry or change causes
> (a) Property to be transferred, paid or delivered,
> (b) an account of the insured, or of its customer, to be added, deleted, debited or credited, or
> (c) an unauthorized account or a fictitious account to be debited or credited.

This language, explained the New York Court of Appeals, "unambiguously applies to losses incurred from unauthorized access to [the insured's] computer system, and not to losses resulting from fraudulent content submitted to the computer system by authorized users."[2] As the New York Court of Appeals explained, to trigger coverage, the perpetrator needs to hack the insured's system and that entry or change made by the perpetrator must cause one of the enumerated covered losses. Or, in the words of the Fifth Circuit: "The policy means what it says:

---

1. Universal Am. Corp. v. Nat'l Union Fire Ins. Co. of Pittsburgh, Pa., 25 N.Y.3d 675, 679 (2015).
2. *Id.* at 680–81.

Coverage under the Computer Transfer Fraud provision is available only when a computer-based fraud scheme causes a transfer of funds without the Insured's knowledge or consent."[3]

Other courts have considered policies with "any computer" language. For example, *Interactive Communications,*[4] *Apache*[5] and *City of Unalaska*[6] considered language providing that the insurer "will pay for loss of, and loss from damage to, money, securities and other property resulting directly from the use of any computer to fraudulently cause a transfer of that property from inside the premises or banking premises . . ." *Interactive Communications*[7]considered whether this policy language provided coverage for manipulation of a computer system that processed telephonic requests for electronic "chits" that were then redeemed for credit on debit cards. This decision highlights the importance of reviewing the requirements of the insuring agreement to see if coverage is triggered based on the facts of the claim. In that case, the Eleventh Circuit agreed that the claim was perpetrated through the "use of a computer" as required by the policy, but found that the direct loss requirement was not met as the fraudsters did not directly (immediately) cause the loss through their unauthorized access.[8] *Apache*[9] and *City of Unalaska*[10] both considered coverage for a social engineering scheme based on emails with false banking information purportedly sent by a vendor. Although there are distinctions that can be drawn between the two cases, the courts reached conflicting conclusions on the coverage afforded by the insuring agreement.

---

3. Mississippi Silicon Holdings, L.L.C. v. Axis Ins. Co., 843 F. App'x 581, 585–86 (5th Cir. 2021).
4. Interactive Commc'ns Int'l, Inc. v. Great Am. Ins. Co., 731 F. App'x 929, 930–31 (11th Cir. 2018).
5. Apache Corp. v. Great Am. Ins. Co., 662 F. App'x 252, 254 (5th Cir. 2016).
6. City of Unalaska v. Nat'l Union Fire Ins. Co., 591 F. Supp. 3d 440, 443 (D. Alaska 2022).
7. 731 F. App'x 929 at 930–31.
8. *Id.* at 934–35.
9. Apache Corp., 662 F. App'x at 254.
10. City of Unalaska, 591 F. Supp. 3d at 443.

1. Other Policy Provisions to Review

Computer fraud coverage is not a substitute for cyber insurance and provides specific coverage for specific risks to the insured's own covered property. This concept is highlighted through the Ownership clause, which restricts covered property to property owned, leased, or held by the insured, and for which the insured is legally liable *prior* to the time the loss was sustained. Therefore, while there may be coverage for property that the insured held in its computer system that was taken through an infiltration of the computer system, there is not coverage for the broad cyber-related losses that the insured may incur as are covered under a cyber policy. It is therefore important to evaluate the claim to determine the property the insured alleges was taken and to ensure that this is property that the insured was holding, and not an alleged liability the insured incurred due to the breach. The analysis can be nuanced and therefore, in some instances, experienced coverage counsel may be helpful to consult as you make your determination.

Computer fraud coverage may also include restoration coverage, sometimes called Restoration Costs. These are the reasonable and necessary costs or expenses the insured incurs (with the insurer's consent) to restore or repair the covered property (such as electronic data or computer programs, as defined in the policy) to its pre-breach condition. The coverage may also cover the costs the insured incurred with the insurer's prior written consent to determine that restoration or repair is not possible.

Experienced brokers, especially ones that work with cyber policies as well, will hopefully assist the insured in understanding how to sort its loss among the various policies it has to ensure that each portion of its loss is being evaluated under the right policy type. However, some insureds may need assistance. Those insureds should be advised to immediately contact their cyber carrier as that carrier will have breach counsel and a whole set of experienced incident response vendors to investigate and respond to a cyber incident. This initial response and investigation is not part of computer fraud coverage and the crime/fidelity carrier does not have the incident response infrastructure that is built into cyber coverage. Cyber carriers are prepared to address the host of vendors and services the insured needs to respond to a cyber incident and with the time-sensitivities required with after-hours and weekend hotlines, among other support services.

In evaluating the claim, it is also important to look to whether this is a single loss or multiple losses, each which would be subject to the policy's deductible or retention. The policy, may for example, include a clause explaining that coverage is provided for "loss that you sustain resulting directly from an 'occurrence'" discovered during the policy period or any extended discovery period provided by the policy. Other policies may use other language to reach the same result. For cyber-related losses, insureds often report these close in time to their cyber carrier, but you may want to ensure that the insured has complied with the reporting requirements of the policy and that the loss was discovered in the policy period (if the insured has a discovery form; a loss sustained form is less typical and has its own analysis).

2. Exclusions

Computer fraud coverage often is subject to several exclusions. These include exclusions for: (1) social engineering coverage (thereby funneling coverage to the typically sub-limited endorsement); (2) confidential or personal information; (3) loss resulting from a threat to the insured's premises or property, or a threat to its computer system operations (this exclusion further explains that coverage does not extend to ransomware attacks); (4) loss of a type for which the insured is legally liable; (5) indirect or consequential loss; and (6) fees, costs and expenses incurred by the insured. There are several cases explaining the fraudulent impersonation exclusion, although this is occasionally still litigated, and there are several cases interpreting confidential and personal information exclusions, which do vary across policies. These are discussed in turn below. The legally liable, indirect/consequential and fees/costs/expenses exclusions are standard exclusions that also further define the policy's coverage and can be used to further explain the coverage determination.

The Northern District of Texas recently issued a decision on a fraudulent impersonation exclusion. In that case, *Blue Compass RV*,[11] the policy used the term "Deception Fraud" for its social engineering coverage. The applicable funneling exclusion was:

---

11. Blue Compass RV, LLC f/k/a RV Retailer, LLC v. Twin City Fire Ins. Co., No. 3:24-CV-1987-B, 2025 WL 1908395 (N.D. Tex. July 10, 2025).

> This Coverage Part Does Not Apply To And The Insurer Will Not Pay For: . . .
> (T) Deception Fraud Exclusions
> (1) Loss or damage resulting directly or indirectly from Deception Fraud. This exclusion shall not apply to the Deception Fraud Insuring Agreement.
> (2) Loss or damage:
> (a) resulting from Theft by an Employee;
> (b) resulting from Forgery . . .
> (c) directly related to the use of any computer to fraudulently cause a transfer of Money or Securities from inside the Premises or Banking Premises;
> (d) resulting from Funds Transfer Fraud;
> . . .[12]
> This exclusion shall apply only to the Deception Fraud Insuring Agreement.

The court agreed with the insurer that coverage fell clearly within the Deception Fraud (social engineering) insuring agreement, and therefore while coverage was available, it was subject to the sublimit of that endorsement and not covered under other policy provisions.

As mentioned above, there are a few cases interpreting confidential or personal information exclusions, applying some of the varied policy language used for this exclusion. In one recent case, *Benoit Ford LLC*,[13] the Western District of Louisiana considered the Confidential or Personal Information exclusion in a policy that had the ISO language in the exclusion. The exclusion excluded:

> d. Confidential or Personal Information
> Loss resulting from
> (1) The disclosure or use of another person's or organization's confidential or personal information; or
> (2) The disclosure of your confidential or personal information. . . .[14]
> For the purposes of this exclusion, confidential or personal information includes, but is not limited to, patents, trade secrets, processing methods, customer lists, financial information, credit

12. *Id.* at *1–2.
13. Benoit Ford LLC v. Lexington Ins. Co., No. 2:22-CV-06024, 2023 WL 6209342 (W.D. La. Sept. 22, 2023).
14. *Id.* at *7.

> card information, health information or any other type of nonpublic information.

The court held that this exclusion excluded coverage for vehicles purchased and financed using false or stolen identities: "The policy provision unambiguously excludes coverage for the loss resulting from the use of another person's personal information as was done here."[15] These exclusions can be helpful in explaining to the insured that while their cyber policy may cover breach notification and related costs, those are not covered under a crime policy or a Financial Institution Bond.

B. Funds Transfer Fraud

Funds transfer fraud requires a fraudulent instruction directing a financial institution to transfer, pay or deliver money or securities from the insured's account:

> fraudulent written, electronic, telegraphic, cable, teletype or telephone instructions issued to a financial institution directing such institution to transfer, pay or deliver **Money** or **Securities** from any account maintained by an **Insured Organization** at such Institution, without an **Insured Organization's** knowledge or consent.[16]

Some courts, such as the Ninth Circuit in *Taylor & Lieberman* have held that this insuring agreement requires the transfers to be made without the insured's knowledge or consent at all; funds sent under false pretenses are not covered:

> This coverage is inapplicable because T&L requested and knew about the wire transfers. After receiving the fraudulent emails, T&L directed its client's bank to wire the funds. T&L then sent emails confirming the transfers to its client's email address. Although T&L did not know that

---

15. *Id.* at *7.
16. Taylor & Lieberman v. Fed. Ins. Co., 681 F. App'x 627, 629 (9th Cir. 2017).

> the emailed instructions were fraudulent, it did know about the wire transfers.[17]

In other policies, the "knowledge or consent" requirement is contained in a funneling exclusion which pushes coverage towards the fraudulent instruction agreement. Some analysis of the policy will be needed to evaluate this requirement. There is some nuanced case law on this issue and therefore, in some instances, coverage counsel may be helpful.

Funds transfer fraud should be evaluated in instances in which the insured's credentials have been compromised through, for example, an impersonation scam, in which a threat actor impersonates a legitimate person or entity through a website, email or through providing "support services." The perpetrator of these schemes will create a lookalike domain for a financial institution or other business, have the insured enter their credentials into the website and then harvest those to be misused. Some threat actors may even tell the insured, after harvesting a credential, that he/she is sending out an access code to the insured's mobile device and request that the insured provide that code. In this way, the threat actor can obtain access to an account even with multi-factor authentication enabled, under the guise of providing technical assistance. A similar scheme can use emails that appear to be legitimate but include a malicious link or a link to a lookalike domain to prompt a login. In all of these instances, the insured will also want to contest the transfer with their financial institution as well to aid potential recovery and to determine if the financial institution may bear all or some responsibility for the transfer.

C. Social Engineering Coverage

Social engineering endorsements are designed to provide some coverage for specific email-based social engineering schemes. There can be some variation across the endorsements and coverage is often (although not always) sub-limited to an amount lower than the coverage limits for the other insuring agreements in the policy. Common endorsements include the corporate deception fraud endorsement, fraudulent impersonation endorsement, fraudulent instruction endorsement, and social engineering endorsement. Although there are several different endorsements available, coverage is typically available for a loss resulting directly from the insured having, in good faith, transferred money or

---

17. *Id.* at 629.

securities in reliance upon an instruction directed to the insured to transfer such money or securities from a person purporting to be an employee, customer, vendor, or authorized person of the insured. The endorsement typically includes the further requirement that the instruction intentionally misleads an employee through misrepresenting a material fact that the employee then relies upon, believing it to be genuine. The endorsement will also provide covered categories of persons or entities that the perpetrator must have claimed to be, which could be an existing customer, vendor, or employee. An entity often has to have a contract with the insured to qualify as a "vendor."

By way of example, the ISO Fraudulent Impersonation Endorsement provides:

> We will pay for loss resulting directly from your having, in good faith, transferred "money", "securities" or "other property" in reliance upon a "transfer instruction" purportedly issued by [an "employee", "customer" or "vendor" as defined therein] but which "transfer instruction" proves to have been fraudulently issued by an imposter without the knowledge or consent of [the "employee", "customer" or "vendor"] [18]

Some endorsements may also have a verification procedure, which must be followed as a prerequisite to coverage.[19] When the endorsement has a verification procedure prerequisite, the insured must verify all "transfer instructions" or all "transfer instructions" in excess of an agreed amount "according to a pre-arranged callback or other established verification procedure . . . ."[20] This information is often asked about in underwriting to verify that the insured does in fact have such a procedure in place, and increasingly, the underwriter also verifies that the insured has a training program in place for its employees to guard against these and other cyber-related risks.

---

18. 2015 Insurance Services Office, Inc. Fraudulent Impersonation Endorsement, Form No. CR 04 17 11 15. Words in quotation marks are defined terms in the policy.
19. *Id.* Some carriers may require the verification procedure on certain forms, such as a bond form, but not on others. It therefore is important to review the policy closely.
20. *Id.*

III.
Claims Investigation

From a claim investigation perspective, for many cyber-related claims, it will be helpful to understand how the insured's incident response with their cyber carrier may progress for background purposes. This section will review in general the incident response process the insured will follow (likely in consultation with their cyber carrier) and the information that you will need to evaluate coverages that may be implicated in a crime policy. Threat actors are constantly evolving, and therefore while we are seeing some trends and have general expectations on these claims, you may encounter something completely new or a unique way in which an insured is impacted by a common cyber scheme.

A. The Insured's Initial Breach Response

An insured's response to a cyber event may vary significantly. Insureds with a more robust cyber-security team will have a well-established incident response ("IR") protocol in place. These insureds will likely have cyber-security teams and committees, and even vendors on retainer to assist with any incidents that may arise. These insureds may conduct tabletop exercises to ensure that they are ready and have practiced responding to different cyber-security threats. For these insureds, there will likely be a set way in which they want to conduct their response, in consultation with their cyber carrier.

Other insureds may not have such a robust system in place. These insureds may have not given much thought to cyber risks outside of retaining a managed service provider for some basic support and following their insurance broker's recommendation that they obtain cyber insurance. Such insureds may be heavily dependent on their cyber insurer to guide them through the process. Fortunately, most cyber carriers have a well-established process that provides insureds with an incident response attorney, who then retains a forensic investigator to determine if there was a breach of any of the insured's computer systems. The attorney then provides legal advice on any notification obligations the insured may have as a result of the breach. The incident response attorney can advise on the scope and content of the notices needed and assist with retaining a vendor to send the notifications. These initial incident response services are commonly referred to as "first party" coverage by the cyber carrier as the attorney is advising the insured about their reporting obligations and response to the event, based on the forensic determination about the event.

If the insured is a victim of a ransomware attack, the cyber carrier will have experienced vendors on a negotiated rate panel to assist. In general, ransomware bad actors will either: (1) lock down a system or information and require the insured to pay for a key to unlock it (this theft model has been frustrated by insureds' practice of having back-up copies of critical servers and databases); or (2) export confidential information from the insured's system and demand a ransom in exchange for the threat actor's agreement to destroy this information (this business model requires the ransomware group to establish a reputation of following through with their promise not to later disclose the exfiltrated information to provide assurances that the ransom payment will keep the information confidential). The incident response vendors will communicate with the threat actors to evaluate the specific group involved; evaluate "proof of life" from the threat actor to see what they have actually obtained from the insured; negotiate a ransom payment with the threat actor (if necessary, depending on the nature of the information taken and the backups available; these negotiations can be volatile); conduct an Office of Foreign Assets Control ("OFAC") report to ensure that the threat actor is not on a sanctions list with the United States Department of Treasury; and facilitate payment to the threat actor, typically through bitcoin.

The insured's first-party attorneys will also advise the insured about their breach notification requirements under applicable state and federal law. These attorneys will assist with preparing and sending notification letters, which are often sent by another vendor. Credit monitoring is often also provided to impacted parties through other cyber coverages.

A cyber event may also lead to third-party claims against the insured. Cyber carriers will also have defense counsel on panel or available by referral to evaluate the exposure and advise the insured on their liability. Those attorneys can defend and settle third-party claims against the insured and may be also completing their work in the background of the claim process. These attorneys and their services are often referred to as "third party" coverage by the cyber carrier as they defend against third-party claims.

In addition to cyber coverage, many insureds, such as law firms or accounting firms, may also have E&O insurance. Some of these coverages may overlap with the cyber policy or even with the crime policy. In the instance of overlapping coverage with the policy you are adjusting, as you work through and finalize your coverage evaluation, you will want to understand the other coverage available and the applicable other insurance provisions in the policies. This will allow you to ensure that the loss is properly allocated across the policies.

B. Coverage Evaluation

When you first obtain a cyber-related claim, you will want to ensure that the insured has reached out to their cyber carrier and worked through the incident response process by engaging the appropriate vendors with that carrier, if warranted by the situation. While the cyber insurer will typically respond to a cyber incident by providing the initial breach response and investigation, there may be instances in which there is some loss that is not covered by the cyber policy or there may be some coverage under the Financial Institution Bond or crime policy.

As outlined above, while every claim is unique, you will want to consider evaluating coverage under the computer fraud, restoration costs, funds transfer fraud and social engineering coverages. In order to evaluate coverage under the insured's Financial Institution Bond or crime policy, you will want to request key information to understand and evaluate the claim. Helpful information includes:

1. **The forensic breach report or other documentation of the breach investigation.** This will allow you to understand whether there was breach of the insured's computer system, the extent of that breach, and the loss the insured incurred (if any) as a direct result of that breach. Due to evolving case law on the discoverability of forensic reports of a cyber breach, some insureds simply have an executive summary, slide deck or other shorter summary prepared by their forensic investigator to avoid creating a report that may be ordered disclosed in subsequent litigation. With the permission of the insured, you also may want to reach out to the insured's cyber carrier and request a copy of any forensic investigation completed on its behalf. Alternatively, you may simply want to make a broad request for any investigative reports, including forensic reports, prepared by the insured, the insured's consultants, the insured's cyber carrier, or any other party. It is also good practice to request a call with the forensic investigator after you had an opportunity to review the report. A subsequent call allows you to ask any follow up questions, address any concerns, and request additional information and

documentation that may be needed including the underlying source documentation for the forensic report.

2. **The IC3 Report.** Most insureds make a report with the Federal Bureau of Investigation's Internet Crime Complaint Center ("IC3")[21] Many policies require the insured make a report to law enforcement. If they have not, you may want to encourage them to do so. In some instances, the FBI may be able to assist with ransomware keys, recovering funds, or may be able to eventually obtain a conviction on the basis of information provided by the insured. An IC3 report can provide some additional information on the claim and the FBI may be able to provide the insured some assistance during this challenging time. It may also provide an opportunity for some recovery.

3. **For a claim involving emails, request the native (.pst) version emails.** This will allow you to better understand the threat actor's use of email and preliminarily assess any access gained to any email systems. By way of background, email contains two basic parts: (1) a message envelope, which contains all the information needed to transmit the email from the sender to the recipient; and (2) the message content, which includes the header fields that the recipient can view.[22] Email recipients do not see the email envelope as it is only used to send the email and is not part of the actual email message.[23] In a spoofing scheme, the perpetrator manipulates the email header to make it appear that the email was sent from a different email address than the email was actually sent from (the email address that actually sent the email appears in the email "envelope").

The below header information shows an example of a spoofed email (in this case, a test email sent by a law firm to ensure that firm employees are identifying suspicious emails). A tell-tale sign of a spoofed email is that the "Reply-To" line reveals a different email address than the "From" line.

---

21. https://www.ic3.gov/.
22. Microsoft, *How EOP Validates the From Address to Prevent Phishing* (Mar. 24, 2021), available at https://docs.microsoft.com/en-us/microsoft-365/security/office-365-security/how-office-365-validates-the-from-address?view=o365-worldwide.
23. *Id.*

From: FedEx <TrackingUpdates@trackfedex.net>
Date: March 12, 2021 at 6:23:03 PM CST
To: Katherine Musbach <kmusbach@grsm.com>
Subject: Package Could Not Be Delivered
Reply-To: FedEx <TrackingUpdates.dcuk2u0@specreply.gmail.net-login.com>

The full email headers can be viewed by going to File > Properties in Microsoft Outlook. If the insured does not know how to send a .pst version of an email, you can simply ask them to drag and drop the emails at issue in an email to you.

This information will be helpful to you in evaluating the email in relation to the insured's loss for purposes of evaluating coverage (and, potentially, for later evaluating recovery opportunities for a covered loss). You can use the header information to evaluate whether the threat actor may have had access to the sender's email system (if the "from" line shows the sender's actual email address) or if the threat actor simply spoofed email addresses. In many claims, the threat actors may have access to one of the vendor's email accounts only and may create lookalike emails for other employees that can be discerned with a close examination of the email chain after the incident is discovered.

4. **The insured's contract with any vendor or client that may be relevant to the coverage, along with any addenda and statement of works applicable to the loss.** This information is important to evaluate potential coverage under a social engineering endorsement, which may, for losses involving a vendor, require a written contract with that vendor (often included through defining a "vendor" as "an entity or individual from whom you purchase goods or receive services under a written contract."[24]) You will need the relevant contracts and other information about the party impersonated as part of the social engineering scheme to evaluate the requirements of coverage.

5. **The insured's communications with its financial institution.** For funds transfer coverage and social engineering losses, the insured may have communications with the implicated financial institutions and may have executed hold harmless letters in an effort to facilitate a return of funds. This information is important to evaluate the loss amount, as in many instances if the insured or its business partner alerts the financial institutions shortly after the transfer, a good portion of the funds may be

24. ISO FI 20 67 10 16

able to be recovered. This information can also be helpful for better understanding the claim and whether it meets the requirements of coverage. Examples of possible requests include, copies of the wire or ACH confirmations showing the transactions, the monthly bank statements, the bank account agreement and deposit agreement, fraud affidavit/reversal submission completed with the insured's financial institution, all correspondence and communication with the financial institution, any IP logs related to the fraudulent login to the bank account showing the difference with the normal IP logs of the insured, and any documentation which ties the fraudulent IP addresses to the actual wire or ACH transfer.

6. **Detailed information and supporting documentation describing the "money", "securities", or "other property underlying the claim, including where this was kept and from where it was taken.** The insured must establish a loss of property falling within the Ownership provision, which limits coverage to property that the insured owns or leases, holds, or for which it is legally liable (provided the legal liability arose *before* the loss was sustained, as is required for the first-party coverage offered by the policy). If the insured did not hold the funds prior to the funds being transferred in a social engineering scheme, there is an issue with coverage. Common scenarios in which there is not coverage include instances in which the insured merely passes along the wire instructions to a third party that performs the actual transfer from its separate accounts.

With respect to computer fraud coverage, you will need to understand what was taken. While seemingly straightforward, many insureds have items of electronic value or property that are unique to their business. You will need a narrative from the insured, and you may have specific questions based on the initial notice and proof of loss that you need answered to ensure that you have sufficient information to evaluate the claim. It is important for claim handlers to ensure that they have sufficient information regarding the property to understand if it is covered under the policy. You will need information both about the property underlying the claimed loss to ensure it is covered property, but you also will need to understand where and how the property is stored. This is because, as outlined below, computer fraud coverage will be specific about the computer systems or databases covered, which needs to be satisfied in addition to the definition of property.

7. **Detailed information about the computer system(s) from which the covered property was taken.** As detailed above, coverage is typically provided for a "computer system" that is owned, leased or operated by the insured. It is therefore important to understand what the computer system is, from where in the computer system the covered property was taken, and how it was taken. You will need to tailor your requests to the specific policy language. For instance, you may ask the insured to describe its relationship to the computer system allegedly compromised, for instance is the computer system rented by, owned by, leased by, licensed to, or under the direct operational control of the insured. Additionally, you may ask the insured to describe the intentional, unauthorized, and fraudulent entry of data directly into its computer system. It should also provide information as to who input the change of data or computer instructions and how that caused the property to be transferred.

8. **Information about how and where this property is stored in the insured's digital environment.** The policy has specific requirements for how a computer fraud loss occurs as well, often requiring a fraudulent entry or fraudulent change, provided that fraudulent entry or fraudulent change causes covered property to be transferred, paid, or delivered, or for an account at a financial institution to be debited or deleted. It is therefore important to understand by what mechanism the covered property was taken. Your requests for information would be similar to those in paragraph 7. Additionally, you may want to ask when the last time the insured backed up the impacted computer(s) and computer system(s) and where the insured stored the backup.

9. **Information about compromised credentials and how they may have been used.** The insured may also submit a claim alleging that its credentials were taken and used to make unauthorized transfers without the insured's knowledge or consent. This can happen through impersonation scams, in which a threat actor impersonates a legitimate person or entity through a website, email or through providing "support services." The perpetrator of these schemes will create a lookalike domain for a financial institution or other business, have the insured enter their credentials into the website and then harvest those to be misused. A similar scheme can use emails that appear to be legitimate but include a malicious link or a link to a lookalike domain to prompt a login. Another scheme, which is more of a risk in light of advances in artificial intelligence, is to impersonate a support service or trusted vendor and have that "support

service" obtain credentials and even an access code to "help" the insured. Understanding the credentials that were taken and how they were taken will facilitate the coverage analysis. A good place to start when drafting your requests for information are those requests outlined in paragraph 5. However, any request for information must be tailored to the facts of the claim. In the case of compromised credentials, you may ask for any information or documentation that shows the threat actor changing any passwords or otherwise assuming the identities of employees of the insured during the course of the transactions at issue, any telephone calls, emails, texts, or other communication with the threat actor where they provided an insured employee with a type of code and asked the employee to repeat the code back to them under the guise of claiming they were confirming an employee's identity. It is always good practice to request a summary of the nature and extent of those conversations or communications.

C. Other Considerations

Some insureds will also request a confidentiality or non-disclosure agreement due to the sensitive nature of the information shared, especially in the breach report or summary. Your company may have an approved template that you can use that provides some protection to the insured, but also complies with your company's data retention and use requirements. Your manager should be well-versed in these agreements and the specific language needed to comply with the company's data retention and other requirements. You can always familiarize yourself with the process and requirements for a confidentiality or non-disclosure agreement at your company to be prepared for your initial call with the insured. It is important to revisit your company's data retention policies if a claim moves into litigation as most model protective orders utilized by district courts have data destruction requirements that you may need to revise or keep in mind during the litigation process.

Cyber-related claims also implicate subrogation considerations. Many cyber-related contracts have suit limitations clauses (one-year suit limitations are increasingly common). You, potentially in consultation with your subrogation team, may want to track the limitations period for any potentially strong subrogation claim as the suit limitations period may expire shortly after or even during the claim process. By understanding when there may be a recovery opportunity and the timeline for bringing any action, you can ensure that you and the insured are protecting all rights. Insureds often share when they believe that a vendor or other entity is responsible for their loss and are typically cooperative with the insurer's subrogation efforts. In other instances, the subrogation target may be evident from the claim presented. While subrogation is not a focus of the claim process, the policy will likely have a cooperation clause, and both the insurer and the insured have interests in maximizing recoveries.

IV. Conclusion

Cyber-related claims are increasingly common and the underlying fraudulent schemes are constantly evolving. These claims present an opportunity to evaluate important coverages and to see the way that fidelity and crime insurance complement other coverages that the insured may have. It is important to closely evaluate the policy language of the insuring agreement, the definitions, the Ownership clause, and the exclusions. All of these parts of the policy work together to shape the coverage available to the insured. For the claim professional when handling cyber-related claims, it is important to tailor requests for information to ensure you receive the necessary information for your coverage analysis. The requests may change depending on the facts of the claim. If you have questions or need assistance navigating these claims, you can always enlist the assistance of experienced coverage counsel.

CHAPTER 11

EXPERT WITNESS AND CONSULTANT SUPPORT IN THE COMPLEX FIDELITY CLAIM—ANALYZING AND UNDERSTANDING ELECTRONIC DATA, COMPUTER SYSTEMS, AND ELECTRONIC RECORDS

Carleton R. Burch
Yesse Yanco
Jonathan T. Rejewski*

I. Introduction

Internet and electronic crimes have taken a bite out of many businesses. The Federal Bureau of Investigation's most recent report on internet crime, provides:

> The Federal Bureau of Investigation's Internet Crime Complaint Center (IC3) has released its latest annual report. The 2024 Internet Crime Report combines information from 859,532 complaints of suspected

* Disclaimer—The following materials are not to be construed as the views or opinions of the law firms or companies of the authors. Nothing contained in these materials is to be considered the rendering of legal advice for specific cases. Readers are responsible for obtaining such advice from their own legal counsel or their own research. This chapter is intended for educational and informational purposes only.

> internet crime and details reported losses exceeding $16 billion—a 33% increase in losses from 2023.
> The top three cyber-crimes, by number of complaints reported by victims in 2024, were phishing/spoofing, extortion, and personal data breaches. Victims of investment fraud, specifically those involving cryptocurrency, reported the most losses—totaling over $6.5 billion.
> According to the 2024 report, the most complaints were received from California, Texas, and Florida. As a group, people over the age of sixty suffered the most losses at nearly $5 billion and submitted the greatest number of complaints.[1]

The insurance industry has responded to the proliferation of such risks and related market demand by developing a wide array of products for commercial and financial institution insureds, including funds transfer fraud, computer fraud, and social engineering coverages. Not surprising, employee theft, which previously represented the largest volume of claims, is being surpassed by a combination of social engineering, computer fraud, and funds transfer fraud claims. As claims are made under these various insurance products, and the volume of these claims continues to grow, it is imperative to understand the technical intricacies of how the fraud was perpetrated and what the associated loss was. Was there a hacking of a computer or computer system? Whose computer or computer system was hacked? What role did this play in the loss? How was the money, securities, or other property moved? Were there steps between the hacking and movement? Who moved the property? The answers to these questions can provide valuable information about the background of the loss, as well as answers to whose loss it really was, and what coverages, if any, are implicated by the events.

Such technical questions often require investigation by experts in the field of forensic computer examination and analysis. This chapter provides an overview of the potential involvement of such professionals in the claim process, and how best to use their input to handle the claim.

1. April 23, 2025 FBI Press Release "FBI Releases Annual Internet Crime Report" appearing at FBI Releases Annual Internet Crime Report—FBI

II.
Summary of Legal background[2]

A. Coverage Overview

It is important to understand the different coverages available, whether social engineering, computer fraud, or funds transfer fraud, including the elements of these coverages and the difference between the three. While all three necessarily involve a computer, they provide coverage for discreet risks. These are not all-risk coverages. As one court noted, because computers are used in almost every business transaction, reading the computer fraud insuring agreements to cover all transfers that involve both a computer and fraud at some point in the transaction would convert the coverage into a General Fraud Policy.[3] Not surprising, there has been much litigation about the scope and breadth of these coverages. Often the discussion and disagreement center on what constitutes a direct loss. Contrary to the language of the coverages, the insureds argue for a proximate cause standard. While case law is mixed, some jurisdictions adopt the "direct" means "direct" approach which requires a showing that the claimed loss resulted immediately and without any intervening events.[4] Other jurisdictions have adopted a proximate cause analysis.[5]

---

2. The following is not intended to be a comprehensive review of the large and complex body of law on these topics. Rather, it is to provide a general context for discussion of the handling of these claims. For a more detailed and scholarly treatment of these issues, *see, e.g.* THE FINANCIAL INSTITUTION BOND AND COMMERCIAL CRIME POLICY: PRINCIPLES AND ANNOTATIONS (Michael Keeley, Toni Scott Reed, Robert M. Flowers, Megan M. Manogue, and Jordan Caralisa Connell, eds. ABA 2023); ANNOTATED COMMERCIAL CRIME INSURANCE POLICY 3d. Ed. (Toni Scott Reed and Carleton Burch eds. ABA 2015), and ANNOTATED FINANCIAL INSTITUTION BOND 4th. Ed. (Michael Keeley ed. ABA 2016).
3. Pestmaster Servs., Inc. v. Travelers Cas. & Sur. Co. of Am., 656 F. App'x 332, 333 (9th Cir. 2016).
4. Vons Cos., Inc. v. Fed. Ins. Co., 212 F.3d 489, 491–93 (9th Cir.2000); Universal Mortg. Corp. v. Wurttembergische Versicherung AG, 651 F.3d 759, 764 (7th Cir.2011); Int'l, Inc. v. Great Am. Ins. Co., 731 Fed. App'x 929 (11th Cir. 2018); SJ Computers, LLC v. Travelers Cas. & Sur. Co. of Am., 621 F. Supp. 3d 962 (D. Minn. 2022).
5. Principle Sols. Grp., LLC v. Ironshore Indem., Inc., 944 F.3d 886, 891 (11th Cir. 2019); City of Unalaska v. Nat'l Union Fire Ins. Co., 591

While incorrect, one court rejected the insurer's arguments that computer fraud requires hacking or unauthorized use of the insured's computer system and held that a loss was directly caused by computer fraud, despite a series of internal actions after receipt of a fraudulent email, because the series of internal actions was induced by the fraudulent email, which led to the transfer of the money to the impersonator.[6] Another court found coverage for Computer Fraud when a spoofed email allowed the fraudster to send emails appearing to be from high ranking officials and directing other employees to complete a fraudulent transfer.[7] While these examples are not an exhaustive list of cases, they demonstrate there can be disagreement over the scope of coverage. In addition to understanding the different coverages available and the nuances between them, it is also important to know the law in the applicable jurisdiction. Finally, given the nature and complexity of computer-related claims, part of the initial decision making when an insurer receives a new claim is whether to retain a computer or forensic expert.

B. Privilege Issues

A claim professional may consider it necessary or helpful to retain a computer expert to assist in the investigation of a complex and technical computer-related claim to identify and understand the exact nature of the fraudulent scheme, the actors involved in the scheme, the movement of money, the steps between the alleged compromise and final movement of money, and other issues. One question to consider is whether the claim professional should directly hire the consultant or hire coverage counsel that retains, controls, and directs the computer expert.

If the claim professional directly retains the consultant, any reports and communications will be part of the claim file and may be subject to discovery in any coverage litigation. Prior to litigation, the insurer needs to consider whether to disclose the report to the insured. The report may provide the insured with an explanation as to the reasons that the insurer

---

F. Supp. 3d 440, 451 (D. Alaska 2022); Interstate Removal, LLC v. Nat'l Specialty Ins. Co., No. 23-CV-0510 (PJS/DLM), 2024 WL 1332006, at *3 (D. Minn. Mar. 28, 2024).

6. Am. Tooling Ctr., Inc. v. Travelers Cas. & Sur. Co. of Am., 895 F.3d 455 (6th Cir. 2018); Ernst & Haas Mgmt. Co., Inc. v. Hiscox, Inc., 23 F.4th 1195 (9th Cir. 2022).

7. Medidata Sols. Inc. v. Fed. Ins. Co., 729 F. App'x 117 (2d Cir. 2018).

is not granting coverage, in whole or in part. It may allow the insured to better understand the insured's coverage position, provide what is perceived as an unbiased evaluation, and allow the insured to see the strengths and weaknesses of the claim. If the claim is not covered but still contested by the insured, providing the report may promote settlement because both parties will have insight about information relevant to the quantum and coverage for the claim.

If the decision is made to retain coverage counsel and an expert through coverage counsel, and the consultant communicates with and reports to coverage counsel, such communications and reports may be subject to the attorney-client privilege or work product privilege. Accordingly, it may not be subject to disclosure to the insured. In coverage litigation, insurers can object to disclosure of the reports by arguing that the consultant was retained by coverage counsel who used information from the consultant to shape and formulate his or her coverage opinions. Insureds are likely to argue that reports by computer experts are discoverable as routine claim communications and that coverage counsel cannot be used to shield the complete investigation of the claim. Specifically, they may argue the attorney essentially functioned as a claim professional assisting with the investigation, and therefore any reports are not protected by attorney-client privilege or work product and are subject to disclosure. Additionally, there may be an argument by the insured that the attorney is a potential fact witness which could operate to preclude them from representing the insurer in any litigation.

Insurers need to balance numerous factors with respect to disclosure or production of a consultant report. In some jurisdictions, insurers may defend themselves from a claim for breach of the implied covenant of bad faith by asserting that a consultant's report showed there was a genuine dispute as to the nature or extent of coverage for a claim.[8] At minimum, the report may be evidence that the insurer took the claim seriously and performed a diligent investigation of all relevant issues.

However, if the insurer successfully raises a privilege objection to a consultant's report, the insurer may be barred from introducing the report as evidence in the defense of the claim or the breach of implied covenant

---

8. *See, e.g.*, Fraley v. Allstate Ins. Co., 81 Cal.App.4th 1282 (2000); Adams v. Allstate Insurance Co., 187 F.Supp.2d 1207, 1215–17 (C.D.Cal.2002); Anderson v. USAA Cas. Ins. Co., No. C 06–07948 WHA, 2008 WL 619004 (N.D. Cal. Mar. 4, 2008); Keshish v. Allstate Ins. Co., 959 F. Supp. 2d 1226, 1235 (C.D. Cal. 2013)

claim in the proceeding.[9] The privilege assertion may impact the insurer's ability to raise a genuine dispute defense to allegations of improper claims handling and investigation.

Another issue to consider with respect to whether the consultant report is privileged is the potential effect of the report on the insured or its counsel. The report may provide the insured with a roadmap to the strengths and weaknesses of the claim or the gaps in the proof. A further issue is that a consultant's pre-litigation report may vary with a litigation position or the information obtained through discovery. This could lead the pre-litigation report to reach conclusions that differ from litigation positions.

As a practical matter, where an insurer's coverage position turns on factual findings made by the consultant, the insurer may choose to disclose the otherwise privileged report to the insured in the claim investigation. This can give the insured a more detailed understanding of the insurer's coverage position. Such an open exchange can moderate the claim process. In appropriate cases, the insured may agree with the coverage decision after reviewing the complete investigation. In other cases, it may give the insured the opportunity to bring more information to the forefront to give the insurer a basis on which to find coverage. Such decision must be made on a claim-by-claim basis, after a thorough and thoughtful analysis, in light of the facts and issues in the particular claim.

III.
Digital Forensics

The forensic investigation process is a critical component of complex fidelity and cyber-related claims. It provides the factual foundation for determining how a loss occurred, who may have been responsible, and whether the loss falls within the scope of coverage. The following steps outline a structured approach to conducting a forensic investigation in the

---

9. Chevron Corp. v. Pennzoil Co., 974 F.2d 1156, 1162 (9th Cir.1992); United States v. Bilzerian, 926 F.2d 1285, 1292 (2d Cir.1991); Dairy Am., Inc. v. Hartford Cas. Ins. Co., CV F 07-0537, 2010 WL 2923895 (E.D. Cal. July 23, 2010); Xebec Dev. Partners, Ltd. v. Nat'l Union Fire Ins. Co., 12 Cal. App. 4th 501, 569, 15 Cal. Rptr. 2d 726, 765 (1993) *disapproved, on other grounds*, Essex Ins. Co. v. Five Star Dye House, Inc., 38 Cal. 4th 1252, 137 P.3d 192 (2006).

context of insurance claims involving electronic data, computer systems, and digital fraud.

A. Initial Triage and Scoping

Digital forensic investigations typically begin with a scoping phase that clarifies the nature of the event and defines the objectives of the analysis. This includes identifying potentially affected digital devices and data, as well as determining which internal or external stakeholders should be engaged.

B. Containment and Evidence Preservation

Containing unauthorized access on a network can take many forms. That said, while the identification and containment of a threat is important, it may be equally as important to collect and preserve digital evidence. While incident response professionals may be focused on threat containment and eradication, there are inherent risks in moving too quickly, which may include, but are not limited to, choosing to restore system backups that may still be unpatched, vulnerable, or compromised. Moving too quickly may also result in failing to preserve evidence that is needed to answer key questions that legal teams, regulators, customers, and others may have about the cyber event.

Preserving and processing forensic artifacts, such as system images, log data, and memory captures can be critical to reconstructing the event. This supports not only the investigation and containment measures, but also future legal, regulatory, or insurance claim processes. Legal and incident response / forensic teams should coordinate early to ensure that urgent remediation activities do not inadvertently compromise the integrity of the investigation.

Incident response teams often assess whether the threat actor still has access to the environment and must take steps to contain the unauthorized access. This may include isolating affected systems, revoking compromised credentials, and deploying endpoint detection and response (EDR) tools to monitor for threats and lateral movement. All this could be done while preserving evidence, and that aspect should not be ignored.

The National Institute of Standards and Technology (NIST) emphasizes this dual-track approach in its publication *Incident Response Recommendations and Considerations for Cybersecurity Risk*

Management,[10] which advises that containment strategies should be tailored to the type of incident and the potential for ongoing harm. For example, in a business email compromise (BEC) scenario, it may be necessary to immediately disable the affected account and notify impacted parties. If there was a fraudulent wire transfer, for instance, this could include contacting banks even before full forensic imaging is complete. In that situation, harm mitigation may be prioritized over the "how did this happen?" investigation step. The answer to the question is still important and needs to be determined in order to complete the investigation.

When preserving digital evidence, it is important to identify and prioritize the collection of both volatile and nonvolatile information. The forensic collection and/or imaging of these systems should be performed using industry-standard tools and methodologies.

That said, not all incidents involve external threat actors or active cyberattacks—for example, in cases such as employee misconduct, violation of restrictive covenants, or misuse of technology. These investigations may not involve hacking, but they still require a consistent level of detail and forensic rigor.

In either scenario, whether it is a ransomware incident or an employee investigation, it is critical that the appropriate stakeholders, including legal counsel, the insured, and forensic experts, collaborate early to determine a proper and reasonable investigative approach to include the containment of the risk and collection of evidence. Ultimately, the goal is to preserve the integrity of the investigation while also protecting the insured from further loss. This requires close coordination between legal counsel, forensic experts and the insured.

C. Analysis and Attribution

The analysis phase of an incident response / forensic investigation is where the evidence is transformed into a coherent narrative that explains what happened, how it occurred, and who or what was responsible. This step is critical not only for understanding the details of the incident but also for informing coverage decisions, legal strategy, and potential recovery efforts.

---

10. Alex Nelson, et al. *Incident Response Recommendations and Considerations for Cybersecurity Risk Management: A CSF 2.0 Community Profile*, National Institute of Standards and Technology, Apr. 2025. https://doi.org/10.6028/NIST.SP.800 61r3. Accessed July 2025.

In cyber-related claims, the type of incident significantly shapes the analytical approach. For example, in a ransomware attack, the forensic team typically focuses on the collection of evidence, containment, eradication of the threat, identifying the initial point of compromise (commonly referred to as P0 or Patient Zero), mapping the attacker's lateral movement within the network, and determining whether data was exfiltrated or encrypted. This often involves identifying, collecting and analyzing system logs, endpoint telemetry, and network traffic to identify indicators of compromise (IOCs) and reconstruct the attacker's timeline. Attribution in these cases may involve correlating technical artifacts with known threat actor tactics, techniques, and procedures (TTPs), often using frameworks like MITRE ATT&CK.[11]

Investigations into theft or employee misconduct require a different lens. These cases may not involve malware or external intrusion but instead hinge on the misuse of authorized access. Here, the forensic analysis may focus on specific user behavior, file access patterns (and changes during key periods of time), USB device usage, cloud uploads, email forwarding, and deletion of logs or files. The goal is to determine whether the individual used company systems to plan, execute, or conceal the misappropriation. Because these investigations often lead to litigation, it is critical that the analysis be performed using defensible digital forensic methodologies.

In both scenarios, the forensic team must build an accurate timeline of events. This timeline becomes the backbone of the investigative report and may be used to support or refute claims of coverage, demonstrate due diligence and generally to reveal what happened. Importantly, the analysis must remain objective and clearly distinguish between confirmed facts, reasonable inferences, and speculative conclusions.

D. Reporting and Communication

Reporting must be understood as a flexible and strategic process. It may be verbal or in written form. Reporting is not merely about documenting events—it also involves shaping the narrative, identifying the audience, and applying appropriate legal protections. Whether the output is a formal report, a verbal briefing, or a regulatory submission

11. Mitre ATT&CK, The MITRE Corporation, https://attack.mitre.org/. Accessed July 23, 2025.

drafted by counsel, the forensic team plays a critical role in ensuring that the facts are accurate and defensible. The claim professional should carefully consider the desired deliverable and communicate with the relevant resources regarding same.

E. Integration with Claims Handling

Forensic findings are not an end in themselves; they may be integrated into the broader claims handling process to inform coverage determinations, quantify losses, and support recovery efforts. This integration begins with aligning the forensic narrative with the policy language. For example, was the loss "direct" and "directly resulting" from a covered peril? Was there unauthorized access to a computer system, or did the loss stem from authorized but improper use?

In ransomware or business email compromise cases, forensic evidence may exist that will demonstrate whether or not a third party gained unauthorized access to a computer system. Unauthorized access may be a factual issue relevant to the coverage analysis. By contrast, in employee theft cases, the analysis may focus more on whether the loss was caused by an "employee," as defined in the policy, and whether exclusions for dishonest acts or voluntary transfers apply.

Forensic experts may also assist in quantifying the loss where digital records are incomplete or manipulated. They can support subrogation efforts by discovering third-party concerns, such as negligent vendors or compromised service providers. In litigation, forensic experts may serve as expert witnesses to explain technical findings and/or to rebut opposing claims.

Increasingly, cyber insurance carriers are prioritizing the sharing of incident response data—the raw digital artifacts uncovered during forensic investigations--not merely expert interpretations. This request reflects a broader industry trend toward data-driven insights that inform not only claims handling but also underwriting, product development, and risk control strategies. For example, forensic findings can reveal emerging tactics and techniques that challenge traditional definitions of "covered peril," prompting carriers to reassess policy language and exclusions. Risk control teams can leverage these insights to offer targeted, pre-breach resources to policyholders, enhancing cyber resilience and potentially incentivizing proactive security measures. Moreover, from a recovery and subrogation standpoint, digital evidence can help establish third-party responsibility, supporting efforts to identify responsible actors and pursue indemnification. While the involvement of legal teams and privilege considerations adds complexity, the strategic value of integrating forensic data into the above referenced carrier workflows is undeniable.

From a recovery perspective, carriers should consider engaging digital forensic and incident response testifying experts early when there is a reasonable possibility that a third party, such as a vendor, service provider, or negligent actor, may bear responsibility for the incident. Timely forensic analysis can preserve critical evidence; establish causation; and support legal theories of negligence, breach of contract, or failure to maintain adequate security controls.

F. Anticipating Litigation

It is important to recognize that the digital forensic or incident response team initially engaged during a cyber event may not be the same team, or possess the same qualifications, needed to support litigation or expert testimony. Much like firefighters are trained to extinguish fires while arson investigators are brought in to determine cause, incident response teams are focused on containment, recovery, and operational continuity. Their documentation and methods, while effective for response, may not meet the evidentiary standards required in court. When litigation is anticipated, insurers should consider engaging a testifying expert with specialized experience in digital forensics, cybersecurity, and evidentiary protocols. These professionals can independently review the incident response findings, validate methodologies, and prepare defensible reports. Engaging such experts early ensures that the transition from response to litigation is seamless and that the digital facts are preserved, interpreted, and presented in a manner that withstands legal scrutiny.

G. Role of a Testifying Expert

While incident response teams are essential for containing and remediating cyber events, they are not always equipped, or intended, to support litigation. Their primary mission is to stop the bleeding: restore operations, secure systems, and identify immediate threats. However, when a cyber incident escalates into a legal dispute, the evidentiary demands shift dramatically. This is where an independent, testifying digital forensic expert becomes critical.

As with the firefighter and arson investigator example mentioned above, incident response professionals and testifying experts serve distinct but complementary functions. The former are focused on operational recovery; the latter are focused on legal defensibility. A testifying expert brings a specialized skill set that includes not only technical acumen but also a deep understanding of evidentiary standards, privilege considerations, and courtroom communication.

Testifying experts are often brought in after the initial incident response phase to:

(a) Validate or challenge the findings of the incident response team;
(b) Reconstruct timelines using defensible forensic methodologies;
(c) Assess causation and attribution in support of or in opposition to claims;
(d) Prepare expert reports; and
(e) Testify in depositions or at trial to explain complex technical issues in a clear, credible manner.

The independence and objectivity of testifying experts are paramount. Unlike internal teams or vendors with ongoing business relationships, a testifying expert must be prepared to withstand cross-examination and scrutiny from opposing counsel. Their work product must be methodologically sound, well documented, and aligned with the legal theories at play.

For carriers and counsel, engaging a testifying expert early, ideally at the point when litigation is reasonably anticipated, can help preserve critical evidence, shape legal strategy, and avoid costly missteps. It also ensures that the transition from claim handling to litigation support is seamless. Engaging the right expert at the right time can make the difference between a defensible claim and a costly dispute.

Finally, the digital forensics expert serves as a bridge between the technical and legal domains, translating digital facts into courtroom ready evidence. Their role is not just to explain what happened, but to do so in a way that is understandable, credible, defensible, and aligned with the broader litigation strategy.

H. Post-Incident Recommendations

The last step in the forensic process is to look forward: to identify lessons learned and recommend measures to prevent recurrence. These recommendations should be tailored to the nature of the incident and the insured's operational context. In cyberattack scenarios, this may include implementing multifactor authentication, enhancing endpoint detection and response, and conducting phishing awareness training. In insider threat cases, recommendations may focus on access controls, data loss prevention (DLP), and enhanced employee offboarding procedures.

These recommendations are not merely technical, as they can inform underwriting decisions, risk assessments, and policy language. For example, if a forensic investigation reveals systemic weaknesses in vendor management, the insurer may consider requiring contractual safeguards or third-party audits in future policies. Similarly, if a pattern of social engineering is identified, the insurer may offer training resources or policy endorsements to address the risk.

From a claim perspective, post-incident recommendations demonstrate that the insurer has taken the loss seriously and is committed to helping improve the insured's security posture. They can also serve as a basis for follow-up assessments or compliance reviews. Ultimately, the goal is to turn a loss into an opportunity for resilience, both for the insured and for the insurer's broader portfolio.

IV.
Examples of Hypothetical Claim Scenarios

A. Vendor payment.

- Hypothetical:

  The insured receives an email purporting to be from a vendor. It asks the insured to make payments to a new bank and bank account. The insured then receives invoices for goods and services actually provided to it by the vendor. The insured pays the invoice for $1 million to the new bank account.

  A few weeks later, the accounts payable clerk receives a call from the vendor asking about the payment. After a discussion and comparison of emails, they realize what has happened and submit a claim.

  Do you need a computer expert?

- Claims handling:

  An insurer may not need a forensic computer expert for a social engineering claim. Satisfying the requirements of social engineering coverage does not require a determination of whether or not the insured's computer system was compromised. However, as a matter of best practice, the insured should complete a computer forensic analysis on its computer systems to determine whether or not it was breached so the insured can take the necessary remedial action.

In the hypothetical above, the insurer pays the $100,000 social engineering fraud limit to the insured. The insured is left with a significant excess loss. The insured maintains the claim is covered under computer fraud which has sufficient limits to cover the claimed loss.

Would your decision whether you need a forensic expert now change?

If the insured is claiming computer fraud, it should have completed a computer forensic investigation to determine the cause and origin of the claimed loss, whether using its own internal staff or an outside expert. You should always request a copy of any forensic investigation. Additionally, it may be helpful to retain a computer forensic expert of your own, not only to review any forensic report secured by the insured, but also to make an independent determination whether the insured's computer system or computer programs were compromised and how any compromise facilitated the scheme. Before retaining an expert, you want to engage in the analysis of whether to retain them directly or through counsel. One of the factors that should be considered is whether the claim appears headed for litigation. Regardless of how the expert is retained, understanding what did or did not happen in the insured's computer system is important to address and refute the arguments raised by the insured as to why coverage is not triggered under computer fraud.

B. Alleged Computer Fraud

- Hypothetical:

  The insured brings a claim alleging a fraudster compromised their computer system and initiated the transfer of millions of dollars.

  Do you need a computer expert?

- Claims handling:

  You may want to retain a computer expert to determine the cause and origin of the claimed loss. You should request a copy of any forensic investigation conducted by the insured. An expert can assist in reviewing the report or conducting an independent investigation, if it appears one is necessary.

C. Alleged Computer Restoration

- Hypothetical:

  The insured claims their computer system was compromised and portions of it destroyed (including the computer system itself or certain computer programs).

  Do you need a computer expert?

- Claims handling:

  You probably want to retain a computer expert. Again, the insured should have completed a forensic analysis of the computer system along with compiling detailed information about its remedial measures. The insured should share this information with you, which will be helpful for your own forensic expert.

While the above are examples of potential claims, the facts of each claim must be weighed on its own merits, and the determination about whether a computer expert or other forensic expert can assist is best considered on a case-by-case basis.

V.
Conclusion

In a world that is evolving and changing, where the majority of claims now involve computer related crime, it is essential in every claim to determine if, when, and how you involve a forensic expert in the claim process. There are many considerations that go into the decision, which must be addressed before the decision is made. For instance, what type of claim was brought by the insured? What are the coverage requirements? How does the insured establish coverage by meeting the necessary elements? Is the insured's ability to meet these elements contingent on forensic information related to the insured's computer system and/or programs? If the determination is to retain a forensic expert, the next question is whether you retain the expert directly or through counsel. Such an inquiry should involve an analysis of many factors including whether you want to disclose the report to the insured or not. As a practical matter, where an insurer's coverage position turns on factual findings made by an expert, the insurer may choose to disclose what otherwise may be a privileged report to the insured for a number of reasons, including providing the insured with a more detailed understanding of the basis for the coverage position. If the claim goes to litigation, you may want to revisit who you need as an expert. These decisions must be made on a claim-by-claim basis, after a thorough and thoughtful analysis, in light of the facts and issues in the particular claim.

CHAPTER 12

THE INTERSECTION OF FIDELITY/CRIME CLAIMS AND CYBER INSURANCE CLAIMS—WHAT TO KNOW AND WHAT TO INVESTIGATE

Toni Scott Reed

I. Introduction

As the coverages in fidelity bonds, crime policies, and cyber insurance policies continue to develop and expand in the technology-driven business world, some distinctions between policies that might, at one time, have covered only first-party loss versus those that covered only third-party loss may be fading. In the context of both fidelity/crime coverage and cyber insurance coverage, carriers continue to strive to meet the insurance needs of their insureds, leading to a growing overlap in certain coverages that the separate policies may provide.

When reviewing the potential coverage for loss afforded under a fidelity bond or commercial crime policy, it is increasingly necessary to immediately ask what other insurance policies and what other coverages exist for the insured, and to immediately seek copies of those other policies as an integral part of the claim analysis. Overlaps in policy coverage are now quite common in technology-based claims, especially those in the social engineering fraud or business email compromise context. The market demand for such coverage has resulted in a number of different types of policies including that coverage, even if the coverage is restricted to quite small limits of loss.

The key concept to understand in the rapidly-changing insurance market is that multiple policies issued to an insured may provide varying degrees of coverage for such hazards. The "Other Insurance" provision of each policy will be particularly relevant to a claim assessment, and it is necessary to understand how the coverages interact with one another and to plan how to appropriately address the overlap during a coverage assessment.

II.
Examine the Various Policies

Social engineering fraud coverage (sometimes also referred to as Business Email Compromise coverage or Impersonation coverage) is now appearing, at least by endorsement, frequently in policies such as financial institution bonds, crime policies, cyber insurance policies, property policies, and package business policies. Social engineering fraud is now generally understood to encompass all types of schemes designed to trick people into performing acts they would not otherwise perform, such as transferring money to a fraudster (instead of a known vendor, for example). Social engineering fraud takes advantage of the good nature of people or employees who want to be helpful, and it employs tactics that cause employees to ignore red flags and take quick action.

Because the losses resulting directly from social engineering fraud are growing, the market has placed increasing pressure on insurers to provide coverage for the hazard, so that coverage is now showing up in sometimes unexpected policies. In these various policy contexts, there are almost always sub-limits stated for the social engineering fraud coverage, some of which may be quite low (even as low as $5,000.00 for some homeowners' or property policies).

In the event of a loss, the broker and the insured should review what policies potentially afford coverage for a loss resulting directly from social engineering fraud or business email compromise. It is advisable for all insureds to consult their brokers to get assistance in understanding the full complement of policies and coverages that exist and to get assistance in properly reporting the loss under each policy that may afford coverage. In many instances, the broker may have the most detailed information about the scope of coverage that has been placed, and the broker may be in the best position to assist the insured with the process of providing timely notice to carriers. The broker may also be a key figure who can efficiently coordinate communication regarding multiple claims that, in most circumstances, will proceed at the same time.

As soon as the insurer becomes a part of the process, the insurer should also ask questions about the scope of coverage and policies that exist for the insured. It makes sense to get full copies of all policies at the beginning of the claim process, because they will be pertinent to the assessment.

A. Study the Details of Each Insuring Clause

By comparison with other traditional coverages afforded under a fidelity bond or commercial crime policy, coverage for social engineering fraud is relatively new. Both ISO (2015) and the SFAA (2019) promulgated insuring agreements providing limited coverage for social engineering fraud losses. At the same time, various insurance companies have also developed their own insuring agreement language and accompanying terms for use. There appear to be a variety of approaches to covering social engineering fraud in fidelity bonds and crime policies in the market today. The approach under cyber policies is often different still. Accordingly, it is not possible to assume what coverage may exist. Careful analysis is necessary.

While it is difficult to describe the approach taken in every separate type of policy available, it is fair to say that the insuring agreement, definitions, and exclusions of each separate policy may differ in the specifics and extent of coverage provided for a social engineering fraud loss. One policy may have specific verification procedures stated as a condition precedent to coverage; another may have none. One policy may have more detailed definitions governing the circumstances where coverage might exist; others may not. The extent of these differences in the terms of the coverage can be vast, so a detailed review of each policy (including all of its terms and endorsements) must occur as a first order of business.

It is even possible that one policy will afford coverage for social engineering under a given set of facts, but the other will not, because of differences in key policy language and terms. As a result, it is important to understand the facts, the evidence, and the coverage language in this context. Step one in the overall process is the comparison of the policy language, including all the pertinent parts that give, limit, or exclude coverage.

1. The Insuring Agreement

The insuring agreement is an important place to start, but it tells only part of the story. As the coverage has developed, insuring agreements have tended to take different approaches to describing the type of loss covered and the scope of loss covered.

For example, in *SJ Computers, LLC v. Travelers Casualty and Surety Company of America,*[1] an early social engineering decision, the court addressed a policy that contained a "Social Engineering Fraud" insuring agreement with a $100,000 sublimit. In that instance, "Social Engineering Fraud" was defined as:

> the intentional misleading of an Employee or Authorized Person by a natural person impersonating:
> (1) a Vendor, or that Vendor's attorney;
> (2) a Client, or that Client's attorney;
> (3) an Employee; or
> (4) an Authorized Person,
> through the use of a Communication.[2]

In that same policy, the "Computer Fraud" insuring agreement provided that "computer fraud" excluded "such entry or change made by an Employee [or] Authorized Person . . . made in reliance upon any fraudulent . . . instruction" and that "Computer Fraud" did not include "Social Engineering Fraud."[3] Those additional details in the policy were important to understand and apply to the coverage analysis, even though they appeared in another insuring agreement.

Another version of social engineering coverage that has been available on the market provides as follows:

> Social Engineering Fraud Coverage
>
> The Insurer will pay for loss of Money or Securities resulting directly from the transfer, payment, or delivery of Money or Securities from the Premises or a Transfer Account to a person, place, or account beyond this Insured Entity's control by:

---

1. 621 F. Supp. 3d 962 (D. Minn. 2022).
2. *Id.* at 971-72. "Communication" included an e-mail.
3. *Id.*

a. An Employee acting in good faith reliance upon a telephone, written, or electronic instruction that purported to be a Transfer Instruction but, in fact, was not issued by a Client, Employee, or Vendor.

For that insuring agreement, "Transfer Instruction" was defined as a "telephone, written, or electronic instruction from a Client, Employee, or Vendor to transfer, pay, or deliver Money or Securities from the Premises or a Transfer Account."

Pursuant to that insuring agreement, coverage was afforded for loss of only Money or Securities (not tangible property), and that distinction is often important in reviewing claims submitted. Further, the Transfer Instruction must purport to be from a Client, Employee, or Vendor, as those terms are defined. A fraudulent email purporting to be from someone other than a Client, Employee, or Vendor would not qualify for coverage.

Insuring agreements that provide coverage only for a fraudulent instruction by an employee, customer, client, or vendor of the insured have been strictly applied by courts, so that limitation can be determinative of coverage.[4] If a separate policy does not have such limiting language, it may afford coverage under the same facts. These are the types of distinctions that are critical to understand when comparing two or more policies that may respond to a single claim for loss.

2. *The Definitions and Conditions*

An additional, and equally important, part of the review is to analyze the definitions that accompany the insuring agreement and to understand all conditions that apply to the coverage. In this context, it is extremely important to check all endorsements to the policy (yes, every single one) to locate the actual applicable language. As this coverage continues to develop, there seem to be a number of key provisions that appear in either stand-alone endorsements or endorsements that revise various parts of the policy.

Regarding definitions, it is important to note if and how the terms "Vendor" and "Customer" and "Client" are defined, and to determine

---

4. Star Title Partners of Palm Harbor, LLC v. Ill. Union Ins. Co., No. 21-13343, 2022 WL 4075048, at *4 (11th Cir. 2022).

whether the facts at issue satisfy those definitions.[5] If terms are not specially defined in a policy, it may be necessary to apply plain meaning principles to terms like employee or vendor.

Limited types and methods of communication may also be specified. Transfers to just anyone may not be covered under the various policies. Policies seem to be taking a number of different approaches regarding definitions, so noting the differences is necessary.

In the condition category, there are often verification requirements (requiring an employee to take certain actions to verify the authenticity of a request by the insured's regular internal procedures). It is important to compare whether the same conditions exist in the various policies.

Finally, one of the most notable conditions that will likely appear in all policies is the "Other Insurance" condition, which is discussed further below.

3. The Exclusions

In a claim process, no party can overlook the important information stated in exclusions. As the coverage continues to develop, important terms are becoming a part of various exclusions of policies. Take care to review all the exclusions and all endorsements for exclusionary language.

A number of policies include what have become known as "funneling' exclusions, which make clear that a social engineering loss cannot be crammed into some other coverage. Example language follows:

> None of the coverages under this Policy, other than Social Engineering Fraud Coverage, applies to loss that is covered under the Social Engineering Fraud Coverage, or to loss that is not covered under the Social Engineering Fraud Coverage because either the amount of loss exceeds the Social Engineering Fraud Coverage Limit of Insurance or the coverage was not purchased.

B. Study the Limits and Retentions

The insured and insurer should take care at the beginning of the claim process to review and understand the applicable limits of insurance and

---

5. Children's Apparel Network Ltd. v. Twin City Fire Ins. Co., 18 Civ. 10322, 2019 WL 3162199, at *4 (S.D.N.Y. 2019).

the applicable retention amounts for coverage. These will likely vary from policy to policy, if multiple policies exist.

In this context, all provisions regarding the applicable limits may not be expressed solely on the declaration page, so review the endorsements for further applicable terms. Keep that point in mind for all policies at issue when you work to confirm that you received a full copy of the applicable endorsements for the relevant policy period.

The two or more policies you are reviewing may have different limits and retentions. Those figures are relevant when it is time to allocate indemnity obligations between or among insurers.

C. Understand and Apply the "Other Insurance" Condition

Each of the various policies will contain a condition addressing "Other Insurance," which will state whether that particular policy is primary or excess to other insurance that may exist. It is absolutely necessary to understand the precise condition that is set forth in the relevant fidelity bond or crime policy. But it is also necessary to understand the "Other Insurance" condition stated in every other applicable policy.

It is possible that both policies (or all policies) will state that they are excess over all other insurance. If that is the situation, then the policies and their limits will likely be analyzed with one another on a pro-rata basis.

Example excess language includes the following:

> If there is any other valid and collectible insurance, bond, or indemnity that applies to any loss covered under this Policy, this insurance shall be excess over such other insurance, bond, or indemnity.

As written, this provision makes the policy excess over all other insurance that is valid and collectible.

1. What Does the Language Mean?

Where there is coverage afforded under two or more policies, it is necessary to determine which policy provides the actual primary coverage, if any. If one policy has an "Other Insurance" condition that makes it the primary policy, it will pay first, and it may have an obligation to pay the entire loss. Depending upon the limit of that primary policy, there may be no payment obligation by other insurers.

In the social engineering context, it is more likely that there will be dueling "excess" insurance provisions in the various policies. If every policy condition states that it is "excess," then the likely outcome is that none is actually treated as excess. The applicable policy limits for each policy that affords coverage would be assessed in relationship to one another, all as a sort of "primary" or shared coverage.[6] For example, in a case involving a crime policy that stated that its "insurance does not apply to loss recoverable or recovered under other insurance or indemnity," and another policy with a similar provision, the court held that the two excess provisions cancelled each other and the liability was shared between the insurance carriers.[7] When both policies purport to be excess insurance to one another, neither excess clause can be given effect, and loss must be pro-rated in proportion to coverage.[8]

When there are two "excess" provisions involved, it is likely that pro-rata sharing of the indemnity obligation is required. Check the applicable jurisdiction's law for any particular cases that interpret how allocation or pro-rata sharing applies in these circumstances.

2. *How Does the Math Work?*

When the limits and retentions for two policies that provide coverage are the same, the computation for pro-rata sharing is simple: the two policies share the indemnity obligation equally. The parties will need to apply more math to allocate their respective obligations when limits and retentions are not the same amounts. Where limits are not the same, it is necessary to assess the limits of each policy, as well as the percentage share of each limit to the sum of all limits to analyze allocation. Because scope of coverage, limits, retentions, and recoveries may all come into play and impose different indemnity obligations on each party, it is necessary to analyze the proper math on a case-by-case basis.

---

6. T.S.I. Holdings, Inc. v. Buckingham, 885 F. Supp. 1457 (D. Kan. 1995).
7. *Id.* at 1468.
8. Cont'l Ins. Co. v. Morgan, Olmstead, Kennedy & Gardner, Inc., 83 Cal. App.3d 593 (Cal. App. 1978).

III.
Communicate with Brokers and Other Insurers

A. Discuss Early and Often

It is advisable to begin communications with the broker and other carriers as soon as possible. It helps to maintain an open line of communication over the course of the claims. One claim may move faster than the other (depending upon the coverage language involved), so both carriers should remain aware of the status of the other claim.

As much as possible, it helps to reach agreement or compromise early in the process about the way that the two policies will function together.

B. Come to An Agreement on Math

If both policies provide coverage, and neither is truly excess to the other, there will be some sharing of the indemnity obligation. Discuss with the other insurer(s) how they interpret the sharing obligation. If you can reach an agreement about the way that the limits interact with one another, and how the math to divide the indemnity responsibility will work, all the better.

C. Coordinate the Various Payments with Insurers and the Insured

If the carriers reach agreement about apportionment and payment process before the conclusion of the claim process (but when each has acknowledged coverage exists), then a good way to cooperate is to also reach agreement about the timing and process for paying separate shares. If that agreement is put into place and confirmed with the insured, then each insurer can pay its own limited share of the indemnity obligation, and no insurer would have to pay ahead of time and then seek reimbursement from another insurer.

Having an agreement on payment process in place will also simplify the process for each insurer to obtain the appropriate release and assignment of claims (limited to their own indemnity obligation) at the end of the process.

IV.
Conclusion

The need to coordinate between and among insurers about a single social engineering fraud loss will probably continue to grow. Thus, open communication will remain the key to making the overall claim process a smooth one. Working together from the beginning will help all parties involved.